Fashioned for Glory

Restored and Equipped through Biblical Counseling and Prayer

Yanit Ross

Fashioned for Glory

Edited by Charleeda Sprinkle.

Contact information: jyross.global@gmail.com

Making Disciples International website: www.making-disciples.net

ISBN: 978-0-578-12480-3, copyright © 2013
Printed in the United States of America

Printed by CreateSpace, an Amazon.com Company

Layout and design of book cover by Kudzai Musumhi.

Cover photograph (from Netanya, Israel) by Reuven Ross.

Layout and design of book text by Reuven Ross.

The sketch after Chapter 18 on page 92 ("Jesus with children") is a work of Yanit Ross (1976).

The sketch after Chapter 33 on page 179 ("Ashes to Beauty") is a work of Jennifer Harvey Paterniti (2012).

Introduction

As a young girl, I occasionally went along on pastoral visits with my father, the Rev. Ted E. McElroy, a church minister in Waco, Texas. I have clear mental images of him sitting on a congregant's sagging sofa, and while holding his well-worn Bible, directing them to the Source of all wisdom. He counseled them tenderly and prayed with compassion. I admired him and his God-given ability to help others, determining that someday I, too, would sit with a Bible in hand and help hurting people find freedom and healing.

For years I have studied Scripture, counseling techniques, human behavior, and books on ministering to the human soul. I have been privileged to attend excellent seminars and conferences on healing. Upon completing a bachelor's degree in psychology, I followed the Lord's leading to South Africa where I served as a Methodist youth pastor and family counselor before marrying Reuven Ross and moving to Israel in 1988. Biblical counseling has continued to be a major part of my life and ministry to others.

As the Lord led me to write on the subject of freedom and healing from a biblical and prayer perspective, I asked Him and myself, *"Why write another book on counseling? Aren't there enough materials on that subject already?"* In spite of these questions, I kept returning to the awareness that God has called Reuven and me (among many others) to prepare the Bride of Messiah (Christ) for the return of her Bridegroom, Yeshua (Jesus), and to the truth that if we are to walk in holiness externally, we must be relatively whole internally.

To disciple others in the faith means to intentionally impart the Word of God to them, instructing them in righteousness. It is to teach what God expects of His people: how we are to think, believe, behave, and relate to others. Although believers may strongly desire to walk in God's ways, often they (and we) fail. We all want to walk forward with the Master, but we tend to trip over the events and experiences of our past. We need healing in our souls so that our past is not prophetic of our future.

Besides investing the Word of God into their lives, we who disciple others should know how to pray with them for freedom from bondages, crippling inner pain, and demonic oppression.

I trust the Lord will use this material to bring further healing and freedom into your life, and that it will help equip you to minister effectively to those He brings into your sphere of influence. God has fashioned each of us for glory; let's reach our destiny in Him! And let's assertively and compassionately assist others as they journey toward their God-given destiny. Jesus is returning for *"a glorious church, not having spot or wrinkle or any such thing, holy and without blemish"* (**Eph. 5:27**). May we be found ready for Him upon His return!

With love for the Bridegroom and His Bride,

Yanit Ross

"The Spirit of the Lord God is upon Me, because the Lord has anointed Me to preach good tidings to the poor; He has sent Me to heal the brokenhearted, to proclaim liberty to the captives, and the opening of the prison to those who are bound; to proclaim the acceptable year of the Lord, and the day of vengeance of our God; to comfort all who mourn, to console those who mourn in Zion, to give them beauty for ashes, the oil of joy for mourning, the garment of praise for the spirit of heaviness; that they may be called trees of righteousness, the planting of the Lord, that He may be glorified. And they shall rebuild the old ruins, they shall raise up the former desolations, and they shall repair the ruined cities, the desolations of many generations" (**Isa. 61:1-4**).

Acknowledgments

This book is the result of God's grace and love shown to me by Him directly as well as indirectly through His people. I owe a great debt of gratitude to all who have helped me: Reuven exhorted me to take the time necessary to write and encouraged me by picking up any slack in our home or ministry that would keep me from that focus. He also provided the cover photo and laid out this book with careful detail. Charleeda Sprinkle faithfully and tirelessly edited and proofread each chapter more than once and encouraged me through conversation and prayer to press on to complete this book; Joan Painter and Janice Whitmore proofread the semi-completed manuscript and offered invaluable suggestions and corrections. Rebekah Beard assisted in typing notes for me; Jennifer Paterniti offered her artistic skills and gave me a sketch (after Chapter 24) to include; and Kudzai Musumhi did the graphic design on the cover. Many others have prayed into this project. *How can I ever thank you all?!*

You will see in the bibliography that I have gleaned much from many authors. Some of those materials I have adapted and used so extensively in my own teaching and counseling over the years that I feel like they are mine. To all those authors and teachers, I say *"Thank you!"* for investing in countless others through your writing and ministries. Only in Heaven will you know how tremendously you impacted people and nations for Jesus.

Over the years as I have counseled and pastored, I have heard many, many stories. I thought I would use some of those as examples in this book, but because I have often asked the Lord to heal the memories of what I heard in confidence, I have forgotten a lot. Those I *have* used, I have changed the names to protect their identities. I want to thank all of you who entrusted me with your hurts, secrets, and struggles. I have been honored to love and serve you.

Yanit Ross

Foreword

"Strength and honor are her clothing; she shall rejoice in time to come. She opens her mouth with wisdom, and on her tongue is the law of kindness... Charm is deceitful and beauty is passing, but a woman who fears the Lord, she shall be praised. Give her of the fruit of her hands, and let her own works praise her in the gates" **(Prov. 31:25-26, 30-31)**.

I met the author of this marvelous book in Pretoria, South Africa in 1988 while on a two-month ministry tour there. As I grew to know Yanit and saw her in ministry roles, I was amazed at her ability and sensitivity in working with young people and families in that nation. Television was relatively new in South Africa when she arrived in 1981, and teenagers were being lured by the worldliness and vices they saw on the screen. Yanit's counseling skills were a timely gift to that targeted group. She earned an amazing reputation throughout the Mpumalanga and Gauteng areas in youth ministry. Her passion for the Lord and His Word, and her love for teenagers and young adults gave her opportunities to share the Lord with countless young people in high schools and youth camps.

Yanit invited me to share my testimony at a family camp of the church where she served as Youth Pastor. During that momentous weekend, I saw her deep commitment to the Lord and her love for others in a way that touched my life and caught my heart. We married later that year.

I consider myself to be truly blessed in having the privilege of sharing my life with one of the greatest biblical counselors I have ever known. This book is the fruit of decades of study, personal experience, and a large counseling ministry over many years. You will benefit from the insights, revelation, and wisdom that God has given Yanit. This book should be a 'treasure of reference' in your personal library.

I pray you will experience greater wholeness and holiness as you read and pray through this manual. These pages are packed with possibilities for encountering the living Spirit of God and giving Him opportunities to transform your life. I know this from first-hand experience as I have personalized these truths, and meditated on these insights in God's Word.

As you read and embrace the truths in this book, may the Lord fashion you more into the likeness and image of our Lord Jesus (Yeshua). May He also give you a desire and anointing to minister these truths to others so that they may find freedom and healing in the King of Glory.

From a very grateful and blessed husband,

Reuven Ross

Table of Contents

Healing the Brokenhearted

Beauty for Ashes

Appendices

ONE

Commissioned as Biblical Counselors

" 'Comfort, yes, comfort My people!' says your God" **(Isa. 40:1)**. *"We urge you, brethren, admonish the unruly, encourage the fainthearted, help the weak, be patient with everyone"* **(1 Thess. 5:14**, NASB).

Biblical counseling deals with human problems from a biblical perspective. Since God created us and knows us thoroughly, we can be certain that what He says about man in the Scriptures can be trusted to be the final authority on all human problems. Jesus *is* the answer and *has* the answer to every situation of sin, pain, fear, and bondage.

Those being born into the kingdom of God today are seldom the untainted, church-going people of earlier years. Today's converts are similar to those who were swept into the kingdom in the 1970's during the Jesus People era. Scores of these new believers have had addictions to alcohol, drugs, food, or sex. Many are from dysfunctional families where they were abused and/or rejected and abandoned. Many have had abortions or were party to an abortion. Several have participated in New Age practices; some have been involved in the occult.

Almost all (if not all) new believers need some measure of deliverance and emotional healing. They need people to stand alongside them as they overcome life-controlling issues, and they need intentional, strategic discipleship in God's Word. We who are called by the Lord's name must be able to minister to them. We need to be equipped to adequately help those dealing with grief, chronic illnesses, depression, and recurrent sin patterns. Being equipped to minister inner healing includes more than just knowing counseling techniques; it also includes being trained and refined by the Holy Spirit.

The Cost of Comforting Others

Before you are competent to comfort hurting, bruised people, you must be trained. That training is extremely costly, because to make it complete, you must suffer.

If your heart breaks for the pain of others and you have prayed to be a healer for them, you will undoubtedly experience great sorrow. Your own life becomes the hospital ward where you are taught the divine art of comfort. You will be wounded so that as the Lord binds up your wounds, you learn how to bind up the wounds of others. Nothing else can adequately prepare you to be the hands and heart of God to minister healing. *"God comforts us not to make us comfortable but to make us comforters"* (John Henry Jowett).

"Blessed be the God and Father of our Lord Jesus Christ, the Father of mercies and God of all comfort [the Greek word is paraklesis–comfort, consolation, exhortation], *who comforts* [in Greek, parakaleo–to call near, i.e., invite, call for, comfort, desire] *us in all our tribulation* [in Greek, thlipsis–anguish, pressure, persecution, tribulation, trouble], *that we may be able to comfort* [parakaleo] *those who are in any trouble* [thlipsis], *with the comfort* [paraklesis] *with which we have been comforted by God...Now if we are afflicted, it is for your consolation* [paraklesis] *and salvation* [in Greek, soteria–deliverance, health, salvation]*"* (**2 Cor. 1:3-4, 6a**).

These verses say that God offers comfort and consolation to all who suffer. He invites them to come near to Him in the midst of their anguish, pressure, and trouble. As they receive His comfort, they are able to comfort others. They can get alongside sufferers in their pain and pressures, and empathize with them. Their afflictions are God's tools to train them to comfort and exhort others, offering them the same deliverance, healing, and salvation that they have received from the Lord. They are raised up in order to lay down their lives to set captives free and be vessels of God's love and healing.

The anointing that was upon Jesus is the same anointing that is upon us who are called by His name and empowered by His Holy Spirit. It is found in **Luke 4:18-19**: *"The Spirit of the Lord is upon Me, because He has anointed Me to preach the gospel to the poor; He has sent Me to heal the brokenhearted, to proclaim liberty to the captives and recovery of sight to the blind, to set at liberty those who are oppressed; to proclaim the acceptable year of the Lord."*

In today's fast-paced societies, we have little time to establish meaningful relationships, so we have few trusted friends to whom we can go with our pain. As a result, our personal problems take on a greater magnitude. Although many problems could be resolved by praying friends who offer good counsel, too many believers resort to seeking professional help from unbelievers. While there is a place for that, especially in cases of psychological disorders and mental illnesses, it is a travesty that there are so few equipped, Spirit-filled counselors who can offer freedom and healing to the hurting.

Commissioned to Counsel

We find a strong scriptural directive for counseling in **1 Thessalonians 5:14**. In this verse, there are five Greek verbs that relate to counseling that we are commanded to obey: *"We urge* [parakaleo] *you, brethren, admonish* [noutheteo] *the unruly, encourage* [parmutheomai] *the fainthearted, help* [antechomai] *the weak, be patient* [makrothumeo] *with everyone."*

parakaleo—to exhort, encourage, comfort (**Rom. 12:1; 2 Cor. 1:4**)
noutheteo—to warn, admonish, or confront with the intention of bringing about change in one's lifestyle (**1 Cor. 4:14; Col. 3:16**)
parmutheomai—to cheer or console the depressed or discouraged (**1 Thess. 2:11**)
antechomai—to cling to or take a special interest in someone, to give spiritual and emotional support to one in need (intentionally getting alongside him). **Galatians 6:2** contains a similar concept.
makrothumeo—to be patient and longsuffering (**James 5:7**)

Ministers of Reconciliation and Healing

As believers, we are called to be ministers of reconciliation (**2 Cor. 5:18-20**). This primarily speaks of reconciling sinners to God, but it also includes helping estranged people reconcile with one another. Further, it involves reconciling believers to the holiness of God by helping them put off carnality and sin and put on new life in Messiah.

We would all benefit from having some knowledge of biblical counseling. Some people are specifically called to this ministry; others give counsel as only a part of their ministry. It is the same with evangelism. We are all called to evangelize, but some believers are gifted in evangelism, and that is their main function in the Body of Messiah.

Whether you counsel as a part of your ministry or as your main ministry function, make every effort to be equipped as an effective counselor. Then when needs or crises arise, you can meet them with some knowledge and expertise. In a time of crisis, you will always fall to your level of training or knowledge.

Helping a hurting person find freedom and inner wholeness is one of the most demanding forms of ministry. It consumes large amounts of energy, patience, and time. But it is incredibly rewarding! Co-laboring with the Master Deliverer and Healer as He sets His children free is one of the greatest joys you will ever know.

TWO

First Things First!

"...be an example to the believers in word, in conduct, in love, in spirit, in faith, in purity" **(1 Tim. 4:12b)**.

Anyone who wants to counsel and pray with others must be adequately prepared. As you read through the 11 points below and pray the prayers suggested, honestly evaluate your life before the Lord. Ask Him to strengthen any weaknesses you have and then form a strategy for developing maturity in those areas. You may need to embrace spiritual disciplines more stringently as well as improve your people skills. Be diligent in your preparations!

1. Be devoted to Jesus and committed to serving Him. Your ministry to others should be an overflow of your love for the Lord. If you minister to people as an expression of your love for Him, you will be able to extend and overextend yourself! Counseling is a very demanding and draining ministry with little limelight. Our reward is not acclaim or appreciation from man; it is to hear the Father's words, *"Well done, good and faithful servant."*

Let's pray: *"Lord Jesus, thank you for Your many blessings to me. It is my joy to live for You and serve You. I declare again my commitment to You today: I belong to You! Do with me what pleases You. I love You so I count it a privilege to care for Your people. I delight to do Your will!"*

2. Live a holy life with a healthy fear of God. Fearing God and hating sin are proportional to one another: the more we fear God, the more we will hate sin and embrace holiness. Engaging in sin reveals our lack in fearing the Lord. Honoring Him will help us confront sin and deal with it properly—first in ourselves and then in others.

"The fear of the Lord is the beginning of wisdom, and the knowledge of the Holy One is understanding" **(Prov. 9:10)**.

The fear of the Lord is our wisdom. It leads us in paths of life and righteousness. When we fear God, the enemy fears us! He recognizes our authority in Jesus when we are under God's authority in reverent submission to Him. (This is vital in ministering deliverance.)

The late healing evangelist Smith Wigglesworth wrote, *"Our effectiveness depends on the power of the Holy Spirit upon our lives and our own personal holiness."* To be able to legitimately show others their sin, we must avoid deliberate sin ourselves. How can we discern truth in others if we are living a lie? We minister out of what God has accomplished in us, and we can only do that confidently when our heart and conscience do not condemn us. **1 John 3:21** says, *"Beloved, if our heart does not condemn us, we have confidence before God."*

Let's pray: *"Father, I want to live a holy life before you. I choose the fear of the Lord; let it come upon me! Remove from me all deceit and hypocrisy. Wash my conscience with the blood of Jesus; cleanse me from all dead works. I choose to live under Your protection in reverent submission to You."*

3. Be compassionate toward others. Ask the Lord to help you to see people as He does. **Matthew 9:36** says, *"But when He saw the multitudes, He was moved with compassion for them, because they were weary and scattered, like sheep having no shepherd."* The Lord is *still* moved with compassion as He looks at hurting humanity. To be "moved with compassion" is to feel a twisting, agonizing pain in one's abdomen. If we are to minister to people with the Lord's heart and anointing, we must have His compassion!

Having a sacrificial love for others is foundational to having spiritual authority over them. We hate the sin that enslaves the person, but we love the sinner. There are times when you should show love with the gift of a holy hug. Dr. David Bresler, director of Pain Control at UCLA, says, *"I often tell my patients to use hugging as part of their treatment for pain. To be held is enormously therapeutic."*

Researchers have discovered that hugging can help one live longer, stay healthy, and sleep better. It can cure depression, reduce stress, and strengthen family relationships. Psychologists say that we need 12 hugs a day to thrive emotionally.

Helen Colton, author of *The Joy of Touching*, wrote: *"When a person is touched, the amount of hemoglobin in their blood increases significantly. Hemoglobin is a part of the blood that carries vital supplies of oxygen to all organs of the body—including the heart and brain. An increase in hemoglobin tones up the whole body, helps prevent disease, and speeds recovery from illness. My 15 years of research have convinced me that regular hugging can actually prolong life by curing harmful depression and stimulating a strong will to live."*

One day, an older pastor visited a young man dying with AIDS. While the two men chatted across the room from one another, the Lord told the pastor to hug the dying man. At first he resisted, but then he stood and walked toward the young man, asking, *"When was the last time you were hugged?"* As the ill man shuffled toward him, the pastor reached out and drew him close to himself. He tenderly cradled the man's head covered with oozing sores against his chest. As the young man wept, he confessed that he hadn't been hugged in two years. Within minutes, he asked how he could get to know his God, and the pastor was able to lead him to faith in Jesus.

Let's pray: *"Lord, please increase Your compassion in me for others! May I see them as You do. Break my heart with what breaks Yours. Please remove any hardness in my heart; soften it with Your tenderness. Thank You for Your mercy toward me; I humbly recognize that it is only by Your grace that I am who I am today. I want to be merciful toward others; please increase that in me. Show me when a holy hug is the gift I should offer. For Your sake!"*

4. Be disciplined in intercessory prayer. Prayer enables us to achieve communion with God so that we are one with Him as His mouthpiece and vessel. We need to be accustomed to the Father's voice, know His heart and mind, and have revelation into His purposes and plans—and all that comes by communing with Him.

Prior to a counseling appointment, intercede for the counselee. More will be accomplished during your sessions together if you bathe them in prayer beforehand. Be diligent to pray for those you are seeing *between* sessions. It is often then that the Holy Spirit will give you revelation and insight into their needs or give you direction for your next appointment with them. Praying in tongues tunes you with God's Spirit and releases His anointing through you. It is a valuable tool in preparatory prayer. It is your prayer life that will essentially determine your effectiveness in the counseling ministry. **Ephesians 6:18** says, *"praying always with all prayer and supplication in the Spirit, being watchful to this end with all perseverance and supplication for all the saints."*

Let's pray: *"Lord, please forgive me for my prayerlessness. I repent! I choose to make prayer a priority in my life. May my prayer life be all that You want it to be. Help me to be disciplined in intercession. Enable me to pray effectively and on target with all prayer and supplication in the Spirit. I realize what I give others must come from You, so I will position myself before You to hear Your voice and pray Your will for those You send to me."*

5. Listen attentively to the Holy Spirit. Familiarize yourself with the Holy Spirit's voice. In daily listening to and yielding to Him, you will become increasingly sensitized to His promptings. You will then be able to recognize His leading as you counsel others. Ask Him to release His gifts through you, specifically the gifts of discerning of spirits, word of wisdom, and word of knowledge. Ask God to enable you to discern the motives of the one you are counseling, and to give you clarity as to what is true and what is not.

Let's pray: *"Holy Spirit, please sensitize me to Your voice and promptings. Release Your gifts in and through me so that I can counsel effectively. I pray for the gift of discerning of spirits, for the gifts of word of knowledge and word of wisdom, for gifts of healing and of faith. I receive Your leading and anointing by faith in Jesus' name."*

6. Listen attentively to others. One of the chief duties of love is to listen. Learn to ask good questions. You will minister most effectively when you understand a person's problems. Don't jump to conclusions; get the big picture before you start giving advice. While listening to the counselee, also listen to the Holy Spirit. He may give you insight that the person is unable to verbalize. Be careful not to insensitively pull information out of a counselee; the natural emergence of information is important in the therapeutic process. "Yanking" makes the person feel frustrated and resentful. Don't interrupt unnecessarily unless he or she is dragging along and wasting time. Sometimes people sort out their thoughts while talking and can reach their own correct conclusions about their circumstances.

Listen reflectively (*"Are you saying...?"*). Make sure you understand the thoughts or feelings. Reflecting content forces us to pay close attention and tells the other person that we have heard and understand. Clarify the hidden needs and reflect the confusion (*"You sound like you're unsure about..."*). Don't allow your preconceived ideas and views to cloud your perception. Discern underlying attitudes and intentions. Be aware of body language and eye contact. Notice what causes them emotional pain or anger.

More on listening

• When possible, meet in a favorable atmosphere for privacy and prayer (not in a crowded restaurant with others sitting with you).

• Encourage counselees to express themselves freely; assure them of your confidentiality.

• Do not ask for unnecessary details of sin, which can be painful for them and hazardous for your imagination. If the details come out voluntarily as part of the "confessing and moving on" process, that's fine. Ask God to sanctify your curiosity.

• Do not show shock or surprise, which communicate rejection and self-righteousness. Look and act as if you hear these confessions all the time. Except for the grace of God, you could be in the same position.

• Be careful not to judge another's problems by your past experiences or opinions. Discern situations by the Word of God and the Holy Spirit.

• Do not touch the counselee unnecessarily. Touching can lead to transference and emotional dependence.

Sometimes you will hear situations that are similar to what you have experienced, and you may want to share your story in order to identify or to help. Unless the Holy Spirit specifically tells you to, *don't* (as a general rule). They have come to you because their pain and trauma are predominant in their hearts and minds. In order for them to hear your account, they will have to repress their hurts and switch tracks, which is an unloving thing for you to require. You can identify in your heart and give counsel out of your experience, but you don't have to relate your experiences to them. They feel—and rightly so—that their pain is unique. Affirm that Jesus understands and direct them to Him.

Let's pray: *"Lord Jesus, please forgive me for my poor listening skills. Help me to be a good listener. Enable me to discern the feelings behind the words and to hear the hurt. Show me the right questions to ask; help me not to solicit unnecessary details. Please sanctify my curiosity. Forgive me when I have hurried people along and interrupted them impatiently. Help me to listen reflectively and lovingly. By faith, I receive Your grace and wisdom to listen well."*

7. Have a good working knowledge of the Word of God. Familiarize yourself with Scripture so that you can easily refer to it or quote it when giving counsel. Memorize key verses that deal with forgiveness, the baptism with the Holy Spirit, authority over the enemy, healing, and other issues that you might face frequently.

It is good to give scriptural homework to counselees (chapters or verses that are relevant to their problems). Suggest that they read and meditate on them (e.g., If a lady has a self-image problem, suggest she meditate on Psalm 139.).

"Be diligent [study] *to present yourself approved to God, a worker who does not need to be ashamed, rightly dividing the word of truth"* **(2 Tim. 2:15)**. *"All Scripture is given by inspiration of God and is profitable for doctrine* [teaching], *for reproof, for correction, for instruction in righteousness, that the man of God may be complete* [perfect], *thoroughly equipped for every good work"* **(2 Tim. 3:16-17)**. *"He sent His word and healed them, and delivered them from their destructions"* **(Ps. 107:20)**.

When you direct people to the Lord and His Word, you are helping them trust God and to look to Him for counsel in the future. Your goal is to make them dependent on the Lord. A new believer may draw from your strength initially, but, when possible, persuade him/her to turn to God. Don't keep counselees coming back to you unnecessarily when they should be leaning on the Lord. Encourage spiritual growth. Each counseling session should be an encounter with God where both counselor and counselee depend more on Him as a result.

Let's pray: *"Father, please forgive me for not equipping myself in Your Word. I choose to do so from this day forward. Open my understanding as I read the Bible; give me a spirit of wisdom and revelation in knowing You. Guide me as I give scriptural homework to those I counsel. Repair their souls and renew their minds as they study the Word. Thank You, Lord."*

8. Have a teachable spirit. Be open to learning from others who are in healing ministries. Allow God to stretch you by leading you into new areas of counseling. Study and develop a working knowledge of the factors that influence human behavior. Grow in an understanding of human nature.

Let's pray: *"Lord, forgive me for not being diligent to prepare myself adequately for this ministry to others. Forgive my pride and stubbornness that keep me from being teachable. I repent of and renounce pride! I repent of being lazy and refusing to study. Please guide me as I seek to learn from others and from good materials."*

9. Have a correct perception of God, especially as Father. What we believe about God is the most important thing about us! As counselors, we must have an accurate view of God in order to be able to correct any faulty beliefs of those we counsel. Develop a proper perception of God the Father through His Word and through intimacy with Him.

Many who need counsel have distorted views of God. Sometimes the foundation of a person's problem is a wrong perception of Him. Instead of believing what the Bible says about God, they believe what they were taught at home, school, or within their culture. Part of your role will be to direct them to God's Word to correct their thinking. Point them to Scriptures that accurately reveal God for Who He is. Pray with them for a revelation of His Fatherhood. (There is more material on this important subject in Chapter 13.)

Let's pray: *"Father, forgive my wrong perceptions of You. Forgive me for the times I've misjudged You and believed lies about You. Please reveal Yourself to me! I want to know You for Who You really are. Secure me in Your love; establish my identity and self worth in You. Enable me to help others find worth, identity, and security in Your love."*

10. Know how to lead someone to faith in Jesus. It's one thing to know prenatal care, but another to deliver the baby! Make sure you can finish the job you start as you share Jesus with others. Learn some basic steps to lead someone into salvation. Memorize relevant Scriptures and a "sinner's prayer." This doesn't mean that you will rigidly share your faith the same way every time and lead the same prayer each time; it just gives the Holy Spirit material to remind you of when you need it.

One afternoon, Joe introduced a high school friend of his to his youth pastor. He had been telling his friend about Jesus, and the boy wanted to surrender his life to Him. But Joe didn't know how to lead him in a salvation prayer. The youth pastor prayed with the teenager, assisting him as he repented and gave his life to Jesus, and then taught Joe how to pray with someone for salvation.

Let's pray: *"Lord, please give me a love for the lost. May I recognize those who are ready to be harvested for Your kingdom and approach them with love, wisdom, and boldness. Help me formulate some strategies for sharing Your gospel with others so that I will be ready at any time to bring people into a right relationship with You."*

11. Be willing to work under spiritual authority and with other members of the Body of Messiah. Be submitted under the pastor of your congregation and/or the person in charge of counseling. Counselors with no spiritual covering can be deceived, go off on tangents, and become prey for the devil. If you are a married woman, be submitted to your husband. Stay under his protective covering.

Within the Body of Messiah, people have a variety of ministry experiences and training, as well as honed spiritual gifts, so ministering in teams is very effective. Where one team member is weak, another is strong. One may flow in some gifts of the Spirit, while the teammate operates in others.

Recognize your limitations and refer counselees to counselors who may have more experience or anointing in a particular area. When possible, men should counsel men, and women should counsel women. Watch out for emotional attachments and romances. Hurting people are very susceptible to falling in love, especially with strong, knowledgeable, godly people. Be careful! Refuse to let a ministry opportunity turn into an occasion for the flesh.

Let's pray: *"Lord, thank You for those You have put in spiritual authority over me. I choose to submit myself under their authority and covering. May I not be deceived or sidetracked as I serve in counseling and healing. Help me keep my heart pure and my mind clear. Thank You for those You have called to work alongside of me. Show me when to refer someone to another counselor. Help me see when people are becoming too attached to me so that I can redirect their focus. Thank You for trusting me in this ministry; may I never betray Your trust! I love You, Lord."*

THREE

Counseling Skills and Ethics

"Where there is no counsel, the people fall; but in the multitude of counselors there is safety" (**Prov. 11:14**).

Biblical counseling is an effective evangelizing tool, as well as a means to help believers and others find healing. Therefore, it is vital that we, as biblical counselors, live in such a way people are attracted to Jesus. As they observe our lives, they should naturally think, *"I want what they have!"*

1. Be easy to get to know. Be friendly! Acquaint yourself with your neighbors, co-workers, and congregational family. If you are naturally shy, ask the Lord to help you to be more outgoing. Choose to be God-conscious and people-conscious rather than self-conscious. Reach out to the lonely and neglected. If you are withdrawn around people, they will be less likely to come to you with their problems. Needy people usually turn to someone they know.

2. Be likeable. People take their problems to someone they like. Show kindness, warmth, and sincerity. Be empathetic and willing to be involved in the lives of others. When you show people respect, you give them courage to seek your counsel.

3. Show interest. People share themselves and their problems with those who show genuine interest in them. Ask questions about their lives and listen intently when they speak.

My parents showed interest in people. While waiting in line or in the reception area of an office, they became acquainted with the people around them. They asked about their families or circumstances and often had opportunities to share the Lord with them.

4. Show competence and skill in counseling. When people want help, they turn to someone who appears competent. When you can, attend Bible-based counseling seminars or courses.

Read good books on inner healing and counseling. Study the Scriptures as your main textbook. Show by your life that you have some answers. (If *your* life is in shambles, people will not believe you have answers for *them*!) Don't present yourself as a "know-it-all," but do be ready to respond when asked a question.

5. Live in such a way that it is obvious you know the Lord. Let others see God's love, peace, and joy in your life. People want and need divine help. When they realize that they need God's assistance, they will look for someone who believes in a relevant, living Lord and knows how to pray.

While in high school, I read my Bible in my free time. Sometimes I was teased and bullied, but I maintained my witness that God was worth my love and life. After my first year in university, a young man from my high school asked me if I still believed in God. When I assured him that I did, he asked if we could meet to talk. After a few times of conversing and my meager attempts to answer his many questions, he surrendered his life to the Lord.

6. Live an exemplary, respectable life. Maintain spiritual disciplines and self-control. Be careful with your words and humor. Never get your laughs at someone else's expense! Speak in such a way that others are edified and encouraged. Be modest in your behavior and attire. Live with integrity; if you say you will do something, do it. Be honest and punctual. Be someone worth imitating; glorify Jesus in your actions and choices.

7. Be confidential. Because counseling is an intensely personal ministry, confidentiality is vital. Do not share the secrets and stories of counselees without their permission unless it is a life or death situation, a legal issue, or it involves serious abuse. Be dependable with information. If people discover that you speak too freely, they will not trust you, and your counseling reputation will be ruined. Rather than breaking a confidence, encourage the counselee to share his/her very serious matters with the right people who can take action.

"Debate your case with your neighbor, and do not disclose the secret to another; lest he who hears it expose your shame, and your reputation be ruined" (**Prov. 25:9-10**). *"A talebearer reveals secrets, but he who is of a faithful spirit conceals a matter"* (**Prov. 11:13**).

8. Ask counselees to report back to you after two weeks. You will want to know how they are, especially if they received a measure of deliverance. Following up on counseling sessions can establish the healing they received previously, result in more healing and freedom, show you what further ministry is required, and convince the counselees that they have value.

9. **Refrain from giving legal, medical, or financial advice** for which you are not trained, equipped, or qualified. Show courtesy to other pastors by not counseling their congregants without their knowledge and/or permission.

10. Live as a disciple of Jesus. Align your motives and attitudes with the Word. Be humble, and exhibit the fruit of the Spirit in your life. *"The fruit of the Spirit is love, joy, peace, longsuffering, kindness, goodness, faithfulness, gentleness, self-control..."* (**Gal. 5:22-23a**).

Walk in the wisdom of **James 3:17**: *"The wisdom that is from above is first pure, then peaceable, gentle* [courteous, considerate, approachable, and sincere], *willing to yield, full of mercy and good fruits, without partiality* [does not take sides], *without hypocrisy."*

"Father, please help me as I seek to diligently build these kingdom characteristics into my life. May my lifestyle and relationships with others glorify You, be worth imitating, and give people confidence to approach me for help. May I draw people closer to You by the way I live. For Jesus' sake, amen."

FOUR

The Counselor as a Good Listener

"He who answers a matter before he hears it, it is folly and shame to him... The heart of the prudent acquires knowledge, and the ear of the wise seeks knowledge" **(Prov. 18:13, 15)**.

Did you hear about the two psychiatrists? At the end of the day, the older one looked fresh, but the younger one was frazzled. *"How can you look so good after hearing patients all day?"* the younger one asked. The older man replied, *"It's easy. I never listen."*

Although listening can be exhausting, it is one of the primary ways we express love. When we focus on what someone is telling us, we communicate our interest and compassion, we build rapport and trust, and we create a relaxed atmosphere that enhances easy sharing.

How well do you listen? Ask yourself these questions to find out:

1. Do I concentrate fully and tune out all distractions and other thoughts? Do I give my undivided attention?

2. Do I make an effort to be interested in what the person is saying? Do I listen for both content and feelings? Is my attention genuine?

3. Do I empathize? Do I try to "put myself in the other person's shoes?" Empathy helps us see from another's point of view and promotes a greater degree of understanding.

4. Do I listen to the meaning behind the person's words? Do I ask myself, *"What is he really trying to say?"* Paraphrasing or reflecting back what you believe you heard shows that you are listening. It communicates a desire to understand the person without evaluating his statements.

5. Do I ask questions, request examples or illustrations, or ask him to rephrase what he said? Does active listening show on my face?

6. Do I listen completely and calmly or do I answer too quickly or impulsively? Do I interrupt? Do I listen to analyze and grasp what is said, or am I thinking of my response?

7. Do I have preconceived notions about what I am going to say? Is my mind made up in advance about my answer, or do I listen with an open mind? Do I check out my impressions with the person to make sure I avoid false assumptions?

8. Am I tuned in to nonverbal communication? Do I notice all the nonverbal cues and clues and decode what they mean? Connecting the nonverbal and the verbal expressions insures more accurate understanding. Do I watch facial expressions and gestures? Do I notice the tone of voice? Do I listen for what is *not* being said?

9. Am I aware of what feelings are stirred in me as I listen? Do I lose control and cut off the person from talking further? Do certain words or topics bother me? If so, my judgment and reason diminish in value.

10. Do I give the time needed for good listening, or am I always in a hurry? Am I available and accessible when needed? How do I handle situations when I do not have time to listen?

11. Do I treat what is shared with me as privileged information? Am I confidential? Do I respect others' opinions or do I judge them? Do I arrange for privacy when I meet with people?

12. Do I listen to others as I would like someone to listen to me?

"Father, please help me to be an attentive listener. May my undivided attention to and care for others convey Your love and healing. Help me to keep my mind from wandering as I listen. Enable me to notice what is not being said, and to discern body language accurately. I need Your help, Lord Jesus, and I receive it by faith. Thank You."

FIVE

Avoiding Counseling Pitfalls

"Give instruction to a wise man, and he will be still wiser; teach a just man, and he will increase in learning" (**Prov. 9:9**).

Shared strengths of counselors include solving problems, relating to people with compassion, and reconciling broken relationships. But there are also common pitfalls that counselors need to be familiar with as they engage in this ministry. A person's strengths can become his weaknesses if he is not careful. The points below are important for biblical counselors to observe and obey.

1. Be humble. Humility is considered to be the greatest and most basic Christian character quality. **Proverbs 16:18** says, *"Pride goes before destruction, and a haughty spirit before a fall."* Pride has caused many counselors to fall into sin. Make sure you remain humble before God. Kneel often when you pray, as body posture affects the posture of the heart. Be gentle with others and reverent before God. Don't think too highly of yourself or of your gifts (**Rom. 12:3**). Abide in Jesus as your source of counsel, wisdom, and grace.

2. Guard your innocence. Counseling is an intimate ministry, and many leaders have fallen morally with counselees. Don't let that happen to you (**Rom. 13:14; 1 Thess. 5:22**). Try never to counsel someone of the opposite sex alone or out of sight of others.

3. Flee emotional involvement. Make sure that you do not create dependence between you and the counselee, usurping God's place in his or her life. In prayer, give the person to God—as often as necessary to avoid unhealthy emotional attachment.

4. Refuse to let counselees manipulate you. Do not let them determine appointments or force you to move into crisis management with them; realize that most people have had their problems for a long time. Stay in charge of the ministry time under the Lord's leadership.

Avoid giving quick answers and fixed ideas about how long the healing process should take. Respond to the Holy Spirit's leading; do not react to the demands of counselees. Do not take sides with them against others.

5. Don't probe for details. Let counselees share at the depth at which they are comfortable.

6. Don't rebuke the enemy too quickly. God may have allowed the difficult circumstances in the counselee's life for a purpose. Work *with* God, not against Him!

7. Resist accusations of failure. Realize that the enemy loves to discourage counselors. You have no idea what hidden, healing work the Holy Spirit is doing in a counselee's life, so don't assume nothing is happening through your ministry to that person.

8. Pray over the details of what you hear. After counseling, quickly pray over any disturbing details. Surrender the person and their situation to the Lord, declaring that He is their Messiah, not you. Resist any temptation to judge. Ask God to heal your memory of details so that scenarios don't replay in your mind or cause unclean or distracting thoughts. Continue praying for those you counsel as the Lord leads, but don't be obsessed with their circumstances.

9. Refuse to take admiration or praise to yourself. Give God the glory for all success in your counseling ministry. *"He who glories, let him glory in the Lord"* (**1 Cor. 1:31b**).

SIX

Spiritual Gifts for Biblical Counselors

"There are diversities of gifts, but the same Spirit. There are differences of ministries, but the same Lord. And there are diversities of activities, but it is the same God who works all in all. But the manifestation of the Spirit is given to each one for the profit of all: for to one is given the word of wisdom through the Spirit, to another the word of knowledge through the same Spirit, to another faith by the same Spirit, to another gifts of healings by the same Spirit, to another the working of miracles, to another prophecy, to another discerning of spirits, to another different kinds of tongues, to another the interpretation of tongues. But one and the same Spirit works all these things, distributing to each one individually as He wills" (**1 Cor. 12:4-11**).

The Holy Spirit is a marvelous gift to us. He helps us understand the Word of God, convicts us of sin, and sensitizes our consciences. He releases God's love and joy into our hearts and helps us see life from an eternal perspective. In Greek, He is called a *paraklete*, which means, *"one called alongside to help." Paraklete* has a seven-fold functional meaning: comforter, counselor, strengthener, standby, advocate, intercessor, and helper. Everyone who desires to be effective in biblical counseling should be filled with the Holy Spirit.

In **Luke 4:18**, Jesus read from **Isaiah 61:1**, *"The Spirit of the Lord is upon Me because He has anointed Me..."* Notice the preposition *"upon."* As the Holy Spirit comes *upon* us, He empowers, equips, and anoints us to minister the life of Jesus to others. If Jesus needed the power of the Spirit, how much more do we?!

1 John 2:27 tells us two facts about the anointing: (1) the anointing abides. God's Spirit is *present* to grant us wisdom as we counsel; He is *always* with us. (2) The anointing teaches. As our tutor, the Holy Spirit instructs us at each point in the counseling process. This does not mean that we don't need to study or seek instruction; it means the Spirit gives us wisdom and specific direction. He reminds us of what we have learned (**John 14:26**).

In **John 16:13**, the Holy Spirit is called the Spirit of Truth. He guides both the counselor and the counselee into all truth. The counselor needs to know the truth about the counselee, and the counselee needs to know the truth about *himself* in order to find freedom. It is in knowing and walking in truth that we are made free. The Holy Spirit functions as the Spirit of Truth in three ways in the counseling process:

1. He causes the counselee to see the truth about his situation. Often people rationalize their predicaments. The truth is painful for them, so they choose to live in an illusion. They may blame others rather than admit their own guilt.

2. The Holy Spirit helps the counselor to guide the person toward revealing and speaking the truth. He may probe deeper with the Spirit's guidance and discern if what is being told him is true.

3. The Holy Spirit enables the counselor to discern the truth even when the counselee is unable to ascertain the truth about his situation.

When we are baptized with the Holy Spirit, we abandon ourselves to Jesus so that He can live through us in power. As we daily submit to God's Spirit, we become increasingly sensitized to His promptings, and we live out the fruit of His Spirit in our lives. (See Appendix H on the Baptism with the Holy Spirit.)

The gifts of the Holy Spirit are available for us to use in serving and ministering to others. All of these gifts are undeserved and unearned; they are not reserved for those who reach particular spiritual heights. Any gift that God considers worth giving is worth our pursuing!

The gift of speaking in other tongues is a valuable power tool for the believer. Praying in the Spirit builds up our inner man; it tunes us with God's Spirit so that our thoughts become synchronized with His. It opens the door for us to move into the other gifts of the Spirit more easily.

When God calls us to a particular ministry, He bestows on us gifts suited for the task. There are many gifts of the Spirit written about in Romans 12, 1 Corinthians 12, and Ephesians 4. Among these spiritual gifts, there are some especially relevant for a biblical counselor. All who engage in this ministry should pray for these gifts:

1. The gift of wisdom (1 Cor. 12:8) is God's truth revealed at a particular point in time for a specific purpose. His wisdom helps us to properly handle a situation or to give instruction to someone about his circumstances.

2. The gift of knowledge (1 Cor. 12:8) makes unknown information available through special revelation. It is also the God-given ability to absorb knowledge that is available in instructive literature. The Holy Spirit may reveal the root problem of a person through this gift, give supernatural direction of how to lead a ministry session, and/or give the counselor divine knowledge of how to pray into a counselee's situation.

3. The gift of faith (1 Cor. 12:9) is the certainty that God *will* intervene. It trusts Him to do the impossible. The gift of faith enables one to minister with confidence, knowing that God is sovereign and will respond as he brings the counselee before His throne of grace.

4. Gifts of healing (1 Cor. 12:9) are for spiritual, emotional, mental, and physical healing. There are many gifts of supernatural healing.

5. The gift of distinguishing/discerning of spirits (1 Cor. 12:10) empowers the counselor to determine which spirit is influencing or operating through the counselee: his human spirit, the Holy Spirit, or an evil spirit. The counselor must discern if deliverance is needed and what demonic spirits might be present.

6. The gift of service/ministry (Rom. 12:7) enables one to enjoy serving the Lord in people-centered services. Those with this gift seldom tire of ministering to others, even when they are physically weary or when the hour is late.

7. The gift of exhortation (Rom. 12:8) is the ability to communicate the comfort of the Lord through one's presence and words, bringing God's peace into the lives of the hurting. It is also the ability to say the right words at the right time, urging a person to make the right decision.

"Thank You, Lord, for giving me Your Holy Spirit. Please fill me again with Your Spirit today. Holy Spirit, release through me the gifts that I need to do the work I am called to do. I pray especially for the gift(s) of __________. I surrender to Your service. Help Yourself to my life. Live through me, speak through my lips, heal through my hands, and love through my heart. May I be a conduit for the life of God to be released into the world around me for Your name's sake, Jesus, amen."

SEVEN

Attacks Against Biblical Counselors

"Be sober, be vigilant: because your adversary the devil walks about like a roaring lion, seeking whom he may devour" **(1 Pet. 5:8)**.

When you are involved in a counseling or healing ministry, you are engaged in active spiritual warfare. The devil usually attacks you *before* you minister to others, *while* you are ministering, and *after* you have finished. You may not feel every one of these attacks all of the time, but most counselors will experience some of them at times.

What may happen *before* or *on the way* to minister:

- Sudden depression, disinterest, and tiredness
- Anger and frustration; strife or tension with someone close by
- Specific incidents or circumstances to block your plans
- A sense of unworthiness, inadequacy, and inferiority

What may happen *while* you are ministering:

- Distractions, confusion, doubts, and unedifying thoughts
- No faith or sense of anointing
- A temptation to override your faith and show off spiritually
- A temptation to focus on the condition of the person with fear, alarm, or doubt
- Discouragement, feeling that nothing is happening

What may happen *after* you have ministered:

- Sudden depression and exhaustion
- Confusion and mixed emotions
- A sense of pride of accomplishment (as if *you* did it)
- Discouragement and failure (especially if healing was not instant)

What you must learn to do:

- Recognize and obey the Holy Spirit's leading
- Minister by faith and in Jesus' authority
- Refuse to rely on your emotions
- Submit to God; resist and rebuke the devil (**James 4:6-7**)
- Beware of the devil's tactics (**2 Cor. 2:11**)

EIGHT

Heart Issues

"Keep your heart with all diligence, for out of it spring the issues of life" **(Prov. 4:23)**.

Biblical counseling often uncovers the influences behind one's actions, attitudes, and reactions. Many people who seek help do not know that their problems have root causes that need to be unearthed. As counselors, we should have enough knowledge of human behavior to discern root causes and be able to surface them. If we only deal with the fruit of inner wounds and sin, we will be unsuccessful in significantly helping the person in need.

Find the Root

A good counselor will try to discover the hidden motivations, agendas, and inner wounds that cause outward problems. Unless we get to the root and sever it, we will only be dealing with symptoms. What we leave buried within will sprout new symptoms and problems in time.

Jesus is not content to clean the outside of our lives only; He also wants to dig deeply into our souls to uproot all sin, ugliness, and pain. He wants to drain the sewers, cleanse us thoroughly, and fill us with His living water. This level of ministry requires absolute honesty. God can do anything for the one who is honest with Him.

In the gospels, Jesus often spoke about matters of the heart, and He still goes after heart issues today. **Proverbs 17:3** says, *"The refining pot is for silver and the furnace for gold, but the Lord tests the hearts."*

The Heart in Scripture

The Bible mentions the heart often. In the Scriptures, the heart is the inner person. It is what makes us different from others, and sets us apart as unique. A reservoir of our past experiences, perceptions, and thoughts, the heart holds all that has entered through our senses.

The heart is a collection of our values, affections, desires, and dreams. It is the root of our passions. In God's Word, the heart is used 257 times for the inner person; 204 times it represents the mind; 195 times it refers to the will; 166 times it speaks of the emotions. What is inside of our hearts will come out in our speech, actions, and reactions. *"...out of the abundance of the heart the mouth speaks. A good man out of the good treasure of his heart brings forth good things, and an evil man out of the evil treasure brings forth evil things"* (**Matt. 12:34b-35**). *"...a man's heart reveals the man"* (**Prov. 27:19**).

Personality is the outward expression of inner character. It is how we perceive our past, experience our present, and anticipate our future. It is the subjective way we see and experience our lives, and how we respond to our circumstances.

PERSONALITY DEVELOPMENT

Personality is the outward expression of inner character.

Five emotional needs of man:

acceptance, security, identity, love, recognition

When needs are unmet, inner wounds result.

Inner wounds

(caused by abuse, perceived rejection, unmet needs, word curses)

Common feelings: sadness, fear, anger, and bitterness
Possible results: damaged emotions, painful memories, twisted patterns of thinking

Messages of rejection and inner wounds create a love deficit.

Love Deficit

We react to the deficit according to our nature:
passive or aggressive

Withdraw (Rejection)

Passive nature

Foundation sin: unbelief

<u>sinful behaviors</u>:
fear, stubbornness, perversion
inferiority, self-pity, insecurity

Outcome of rejection complex:
despair, suicide

Attack (Rebellion)

Aggressive nature

Foundation sin: pride

<u>sinful behaviors</u>:
violence, conceit, criticism
witchcraft, manipulation

Outcome of rebellion complex:
hatred, murder

As born-again believers, we can ask God to fill our love deficit with His love.

Allow God's Love to Fill the Deficit

Find security and completeness in the love of God the Father.
Put off the old self and put on the new self in Jesus.
Grow in inner wholeness and outer holiness.

Until we allow the Holy Spirit to transform us, our personality will reflect the sum total of three things: our reactions to all that we have experienced, all that has entered our senses, and how we perceive others and ourselves. *The events we remember the most have shaped us the most.*

When we come into the kingdom of God, we are far from what God intends us to be. Wounded by life, we arrive broken, hurt, angry, and self-centered. God lovingly begins to clean us up and to bring beauty out of our ashes. We grow into our new life with the Holy Spirit's help, intentionally putting off the old nature and putting on the new. Because sin carries a death sentence, God, in His mercy, reveals our sin to us so that we can confess it and repent. He wants to cleanse us and fill us with His Spirit so that rivers of living water will flow from us, rather than streams of polluted water.

"Strip yourselves of your former nature—put off and discard your old, unrenewed self—which characterized your previous manner of life; and be constantly renewed in the spirit of your mind—have a fresh mental and spiritual attitude; and put on the new nature (the regenerate self) created in God's image, (Godlike) in true righteousness and holiness" (**Eph. 4:22-24**, Amplified Bible).

Problems, needs, and fears

Many of our problems began when we were children. In those formative years, we began shaping our values and developing our personalities. We are born with five emotional needs that must be met in order for us to feel loved and esteemed: acceptance, security, identity, love, and recognition. When one of these five needs is not met, we interpret that as a message of rejection, and an inner wound results. Our deepest fear is that our human needs will not be met, so we grow up with some degree of fear of abandonment and rejection. Rejection is the feeling of being unwanted, excluded, and worthless.

Our deepest hurts come from those closest to us—our family members and respected authority figures (pastors, teachers, coaches). The father influences his child's identity the most. He enables girls to feel safe and protected and boys to feel strong. The presence or absence of an engaged, loving father is *the* determining factor for teenagers who get pregnant, go to prison, or are juvenile delinquents. Their race, where they live, and their economic status have less influence than does their father.

As we perceive messages of rejection (we all do because no parent is perfect), we begin to develop a love deficit. We interpret rejection to be a lack of love. The love deficit influences our personality. The way we handle pain and rejection will determine how we relate to our world and future.

Passive or Aggressive Nature

We are born with a passive or an aggressive human nature. We respond to the love deficit and to current hurts according to our nature.

If we are of a *passive nature*, we react by withdrawing from further pain. If we have an *aggressive nature*, we react by attacking, or lashing out in anger.

God's plan was and is that we would give our pain to Him and receive His love to heal our hearts. The needs of the heart are greater than the power and ability of human love to heal. We need to know God's love which far outweighs the heaviest hurts we carry; it alone has the power to restore our souls! We have all been hurt and have a love deficit that only His love can fill.

A True Story

Some years ago in South America, a father was estranged from his adult son, Paco. After many years passed, he regretted that they had no relationship and realized that life was too short to maintain such a separation. He began to deeply desire restoration with Paco, yet he didn't know where he was or how to find him. Finally, the elderly man put an ad in the regional newspaper, which read, *"Paco, all is forgiven. I want to be reconciled to you. Please meet me on the steps of the county court house on Monday morning at 10. I love you. Your father."* On that morning, over 300 men named Paco arrived at the county court house steps.

How desperately we all need the expressed love of a father! And how very comforting and healing it is to know that when our own fathers cannot or will not give us the love we need, that our heavenly Father is ready with outstretched arms to receive us.

"For this reason I bow my knees to the Father of our Lord Jesus Christ, from whom the whole family in heaven and earth is named, that He would grant you, according to the riches of His glory, to be strengthened with might through His Spirit in the inner man, that Christ may dwell in your hearts through faith; that you, being rooted and grounded in love, may be able to comprehend with all the saints what is the width and length and depth and height—to know the love of Christ which passes knowledge; that you may be filled with all the fullness of God" **(Eph. 3:14-20)**.

NINE

The Rejection Complex

"For You formed my inward parts; You covered me in my mother's womb. I will praise You, for I am fearfully and wonderfully made; marvelous are Your works, and that my soul knows very well. My frame was not hidden from You, when I was made in secret, and skillfully wrought in the lowest parts of the earth. Your eyes saw my substance, being yet unformed. And in Your book they all were written, the days fashioned for me, when as yet there were none of them" **(Ps. 139:13-16)**.

As King David wrote in Psalm 139, the Lord formed us while we were in the womb. Each of us is His intricate design, fashioned for His pleasure, purposes, and glory. Our passive or aggressive nature is included in that design.

Those who are born with a passive nature will react to messages of rejection by shrinking back. Perceived or real rejection causes them to withdraw further to avoid more pain. They feel worthless and inferior. If wounds of rejection are not healed with acceptance and love relatively quickly, they can take root in one's heart and germinate a series of emotional and mental reactions that develop into a rejection complex.

A Wicked Heart of Unbelief

Deeply rooted in the heart of the person with rejection issues is a *"wicked heart of unbelief in departing from the living God"* **(Hebrews 3:12)**. Unbelief is choosing to believe what past experiences or observations have communicated to us rather than what God's Word tells us.

John's father often told him, *"You'll never amount to anything! No one will ever love you!"* John believed his father's words, and they became curses to him. He made foolish mistakes and wasn't loved by anyone in particular. But one day he heard of God's unconditional love for him; he learned that Jesus died and rose again, triumphing over death and hell so that he could be saved.

John heard that God chose him from the foundation of the world, and that he was precious to Him. At that point, John faced a dilemma. If he believed his father's harsh words and the messages of his experiences in life, he would be guilty of unbelief and of rejecting God's Truth. But if he believed God's Word, what would he do with the facts of his life? John chose to believe God, choosing a walk of faith and trust in Him. He prayed over his past, breaking word curses, forgiving his father, and praying for healing over the wounds in his soul. In time, John was free and learned to walk strong in grace.

If our past is riddled with rejection, and we perceive ourselves as worthless even though God's Word says we are precious, we are guilty of unbelief. Will we believe the lies of the enemy or the truth of God's Word? No matter how we are treated by others, because God says we have value, we do! If we are beset with rejection and unbelief, it will show up in our emotions, thought patterns, and spirit. Ask the Holy Spirit to show you what evidences of rejection are in your life. Then ask Him to excavate and restore your soul.

Evidences of Unbelief in the Emotions

1. unhappiness, dejection — Sustained mourning or sorrow over a long period of time can open a door to a spirit of heaviness, which fosters further sadness and depression and can attract more rejection.

2. self-pity — When we are grieved or disappointed, we tend to console and pity ourselves. Self-pity exhibits and enhances rejection and misery. (To abort self-pity, walk in the opposite spirit of thankfulness.)

3. self-loathing — In comparing ourselves with others, we don't feel like we measure up, so we reject ourselves (e.g., "I'm not as smart as others."). Because we are critical of ourselves, we are tempted to criticize others as well. Our low self-image may eventually cause us to be self-destructive.

A primary cause of self-loathing is rejection. When people reject us (especially when we are young and impressionable), we tend to reject ourselves. We hate the part of us that is ridiculed and discarded.

If they mock our lack of athletic ability, we may develop a hatred of our bodies. If they mock our academic performance, we may reject our mental abilities. If they say we are ugly, we may despise our appearance.

Illicit sexual activity can also cause self-contempt. Whether it is imposed upon us, such as in cases of incest, molestation or rape, or whether we have engaged purposely in immorality, the self-blame and depreciation of worth can mature into self-hatred.

Victims of anorexia and bulimia often reject themselves because they hate their bodies or their circumstances. They may react to feelings of inferiority, guilt, or anger by overeating or refusing to eat. Most food addicts point back to wounds of rejection (or perceived rejection), overwhelming circumstances, or unresolved grief as the cause of their addiction. The emotion experienced with self-loathing is shame; it is a feeling of intense humiliation. Self-hatred can give the spirit of death a foothold in a person's life.

4. depression, despair — Indicators of depression include a loss of vitality and energy, a tired and sad countenance, a withdrawal from social life, a decline of activity at work and home, a difficulty in concentration, and feelings of guilt and self-reproach. Depression is the feeling of being on the brink of a bottomless pit and lacking the energy to move away from the edge. Occasional depression is normal; regular or chronic depression is not.

5. indifference, lethargy — Common thoughts and comments of those who feel apathetic are: *What's the use? I'll always be like this!* It is passionless existence.

Evidences of Unbelief in the Mind

1. inferiority — Frequent rejection causes one to believe he is not of the same caliber as others; he believes he is inferior.

2. insecurity — The belief that we are not safe or protected can result in insecurity. We may feel anxious, threatened, or out of control, and react explosively rather than respond sensibly. We may feel helpless and be defensive and distrusting.

3. inadequacy, fear of failure — Rejection can cause us to believe we are inadequate. Fearing failure, we seldom take on new challenges (including relationships of commitment). People controlled by a fear of failure believe what they do determines who they are so they believe it is better not to try than to try and possibly fail.

4. false guilt — When we take responsibility or blame that does not belong to us, we feel inappropriately at fault for another's pain or failure.

5. fantasy — Hurting people often daydream a situation or a life that they prefer to their own. In the fantasies, they are central, receiving the attention and love that they long to have. Common fantasies are the "suffering hero" and the "conquering hero." Sexual fantasies are also common.

6. loneliness, jealousy, envy — Longing for intimacy causes one to covet the relationships of others. Once jealousy has intensified to envy, it can invite a spirit of murder. Jealousy and envy are not simple sins that can be easily shrugged off. They must be repented of, confessed, and renounced. *"...for love is as strong as death, jealousy as cruel as the grave; its flames are flames of fire, a most vehement flame"* (**Song of Sol. 8:6b**).

Evidences of Unbelief in the Human Spirit

1. withdrawal, hopelessness — One of the basic functions of the human spirit is to sustain life. When rejection settles into our spirit, we begin to withdraw increasingly from life into hopelessness and despair. *"I would have lost heart* [despaired] *unless I had believed that I would see the goodness of the Lord in the land of the living"* (**Ps. 27:13**).

2. negative, defeated — Depression in advanced stages renders one's spirit incapable of sustaining life emotionally or physically. There is no energy to perform, no joy, no drive, no interest, no lust, no greed, no humor; the person is emotionally bankrupt.

A depressed person cannot help himself; he must be helped out of the pit. He is dependent on the love, prayers, and involvement of friends. He might also need medication temporarily to increase and sustain the serotonin levels in his brain.

3. death wish — Once death has settled into a person's spirit, he may attempt suicide or give up the will to live. Wishing for or praying for death is an invitation to the spirit of death. It gives a foothold to the enemy to inflict illness, injury, an untimely death, or a gradual decline in health. Death wishes must be confessed and renounced.

For a few years, I had frequent health problems that ranged from moderate to serious. As I desperately sought God, He revealed to me that I had a death wish. It originated nine years prior when, as a teenager, I believed my father's death was my fault. I believed if I had died, he could have lived. I considered his life far more valuable than mine. Although I did not actually wish to die, I believed I didn't deserve to live. The spirit of death was attacking my health, hope, joy, and destiny. I repented of believing the enemy's lies about my father's death being my fault. Then I renounced and rebuked the spirit of death, and declared **Psalm 118:17**, *"I shall not die, but live, and declare the works of the Lord."* From that point onward, my health began to improve.

Distinctive Behaviors of Rejection

1. emotional immaturity and regressive behavior — When we suffer the breakdown of a primary relationship early in life, we get stuck emotionally. Later, when we experience stresses or crises, we tend to react in an infantile or immature manner.

Infantile reactions are those you would expect to see in a child but not in an adult. They include rage (slamming doors, kicking a dog, beating a child), denial and fantasy (not accepting reality, daydreaming a preferable reality), false guilt (taking on blame that is not his), childish fears, moodiness, and regression to childish behavior of all sorts (such as hiding under the bed).

Lisa wanted counseling and healing for her rejection issues and corresponding behaviors. She had been severely abused by her mother when she was a child, often locked in a small chicken shed for hours at a time without food or warmth. As an adult, when she felt insecure or anxious, she would sit in a rocking chair, suck her thumb, and hug a teddy bear. She was showing regressive behavior.

Emotional immaturity is a result of unforgiveness. At the time of the hurt and breakdown of the relationship, emotional growth stops. When forgiveness is given, the emotional growth resumes. The person then usually matures fairly quickly to the place of his or her chronological age.

2. filling the love deficit with someone or something — Trying to fill the love vacuum inside, we may set our affections on someone beyond what is acceptable. This can result in emotional dependency and lead to smothering, possessing, manipulating, and/or worshipping that person. No human relationship can hold up under that kind of pressure, so it eventually breaks down. Rejection follows, and the cycle continues.

Some people try to fill their love deficit with religion, a career, possessions, intellectualism, sex, or pleasure. Anything that we set our affection on to fill our love-hunger or to numb inner pain will disappoint us. Only God's unconditional love is able to fill the human love vacuum.

3. loss of self-identity — When we feel rejected, we become unsure of who we are or for what purpose God created us. This negatively affects our performance at school, work, or church; it can cause us to neglect or reject our natural gifts or talents.

At the point of major rejection, we will frequently alienate the part of us that was rejected. If the rejection was connected to our sexuality, we may experience gender confusion and practice cross-dressing or homosexuality.

God made us to find our identities in Him, but when we are distant from Him, we search for identity through what the world has to offer.

Teenagers may try to be like their peers and participate in drinking alcohol, smoking, taking drugs, and/or engaging in immorality. Young people may find their identities in their music, appearance, or worldly possessions.

Adults look for identity in their careers, the achievements of their children, and/or in church activities. In full-gospel circles, people may search for identity through their spiritual gifts and ministries. When someone finds his identity in his work, any rejection of his efforts he takes as personal rejection. He is not able to separate the rejection of his work from rejection of himself. He may feel sick inside, depressed or despondent, and his self-talk may be critical and destructive (e.g., *"Of course, he doesn't like my work!" "Why do I try?"*)

Common lies we believe about our identity are: (1) "No one would love me if they really knew me." (2) "I am unworthy and undeserving." (3) "If I don't find a way to meet my needs, they will never be met. I can't trust God to meet them." Because we believe these lies, our lack of identity may lead us into depression or sin. We must find our identity in God. As we develop an intimate relationship with Him, we will find identity and security.

4. unstable relationship with God — Another result of the rejection complex is the tendency to relate to God on the basis of works, trying to earn His love and acceptance. We cannot understand unconditional love and grace, having not had it or believed it even if we *did* experience it. So, we become "performance-oriented" to earn the love, approval, and acceptance of God, others, and ourselves. We believe we must meet certain standards in order to feel good about ourselves. We must DO because our BEING is not enough.

From the wounds in our souls, we perceive ourselves as being rejected and unworthy, so we strive to earn approval. We perform for love and acceptance, believing that love is given only when deserved. As a result, we love others conditionally. This problem in congregations or homes creates strife, control, and competition. Consequences of this false belief system include fearing failure, being a perfectionist and driven to succeed, manipulating others to achieve success, and withdrawing from healthy risks.

Western cultures feed this problem by emphasizing achievement and performance. Living with conditional love and competition, we struggle to believe in God's free grace. We enter into salvation by grace, and yet we often try to stay in God's favor by works! *"...Did you receive the Spirit by the works of the law, or by the hearing of faith? Are you so foolish? Having begun in the Spirit, are you now being made perfect by the flesh?"* **(Gal. 3:2b-3)**

There is nothing we can do to earn God's acceptance or approval; Jesus did it all! We need to humbly accept His free gift of salvation and grace. We must counteract the lies about our worthlessness with the truth of justification, which can be expressed this way: *"Because of Jesus Christ's righteousness, I am pleasing to the Father"* (**Rom. 5:1**). Breaking free from a performance orientation requires us to believe in God's unconditional love for us, and to willingly offer that love to others.

When praying for someone with a rejection complex, you might feel led by the Holy Spirit to ask the person to remember a significant scene of rejection from his past. Then ask Jesus to enter the scene where He can minister His love, forgiveness, and healing to him, setting him free to believe in and experience God's love.

1 John 4:16 says, *"And we have known and believed the love that God has to us. God is love; and he who abides in love, abides in God and God in him."* We need to know God's love with our minds and believe it in our hearts. It's not enough to merely give mental assent to God's nature of love; we also need to believe His love for us personally in order for the wounds of rejection and abandonment to be healed.

5. unable to give and receive love — A final behavioral pattern common for those with a rejection complex is the inability to give and receive love. The fear of rejection holds us captive. We do not trust easily, and we expect ulterior motives when someone affirms us or is kind to us.

The wounded are not to blame for the hurt and rejection they have received, but they *are* responsible for their responses! Many have built walls around their hearts for safety, but those walls also barricade them within a self-made prison.

Inside the walls, they feel lonely, insecure, and afraid. They can continue living in rejection and fear, or they can forgive and learn to trust again.

Action to Take

Reread the list of evidences of rejection and see if any apply to you. Be honest in your self-evaluation. Repent of and renounce unbelief and the evidences of unbelief that you see in your emotions, mind, and spirit. Now look at the behavioral patterns of the rejection complex. Pray thoroughly through any of the behaviors that describe you.

This is a good beginning to finding freedom from rejection. However, rejection is usually deeply embedded in one's soul and not quickly overcome. Therefore, more extensive help is offered in the next chapter.

TEN

Freedom from Rejection

"The voice of one crying in the wilderness: 'Prepare the way of the Lord; make straight in the desert a highway for our God. Every valley shall be exalted...the crooked places shall be made straight and the rough places smooth; the glory of the Lord shall be revealed...' " **(Isa. 40:3-5a)**.

Rejection is considered to be the deepest and most common wound the human spirit ever has to endure. Everyone has experienced rejection at some level. Our most agonizing hurts come from family members and authority figures; when the family member is also an authority figure (like parents or grandparents), the rejection can be particularly devastating.

Unbelief finds a place in our hearts when rejection finds a sure footing in our lives. Unbelief is choosing to look at the visible over the invisible, the natural over the supernatural, and past experiences over God's Word. In order to find freedom from unbelief and the destruction of rejection, there are certain steps a person can take.

Steps to Freedom

1. Forgive everyone who has hurt or rejected you. Forgiveness is often a layered process; we forgive one layer at a time. Choose to forgive as fully as possible, but know that you may find later that you need to forgive again on a deeper level, and then again, on an even deeper level. Continue to forgive and bless those who hurt you until you can think of them with no emotional pain. We forgive to the degree that we feel the pain, so the next step may be crucial as you let go of past grievances.

2. Give all the hurt and rejection to Jesus, and ask Him to heal your wounds. You might feel the hurt again as God touches the memories and emotions. Grieve all pain and losses. Don't hold back or feel guilty about expressing your emotions; doing so is a natural part of the healing process.

3. Believe that you are fully accepted by the Father, the Son, and the Holy Spirit. **Ephesians 1:6b** says, *"...He made us accepted in the Beloved."* The Greek word translated "accepted" in this verse is the same word in Luke 1:28 translated "highly favored one." When you come to God through Jesus, you are as accepted and highly favored as Jesus Himself. You become a member of God's family, and He loves you as much as He loves Jesus!

The divine antidote to rejection and unbelief is intimacy with God. As you hear His voice, feed on His Word, and experience His presence while worshiping Him, you will experience healing. Cultivate a close relationship with the Lord, and you will be established in security. While believing and receiving God's love, you will move from unbelief to faith and from fear to peace.

4. Find your identity in Jesus. Learn what the Word of God says about you. For instance, you are made in His image (**2 Cor. 3:18**); you are His workmanship/masterpiece (**Eph. 2:10**); you are a new creation (**2 Cor. 5:17**). You are superior to no one and inferior to no one; you are in Messiah (see Appendix C). Counteract the lies of the devil about your worth with the truth of Scripture. Read the Bible as a love letter of absolute truth to you; resist the spirit of unbelief if you question God's Word. Reading the Bible aloud will increase your faith. *"Faith comes by hearing, and hearing by the Word of God"* (**Rom. 10:17**).

5. Break harmful promises and oaths. Many children make promises at the time of wounding to protect themselves from more hurt. These promises hold them captive. In Jesus' name, break every childhood oath that has held you captive, asking the Lord's forgiveness for making those oaths (e.g., *"I'll never show my true feelings again." "I will never trust men!"*).

6. Receive the Father's love and forgiveness. Accept God's grace, resist condemnation, and walk free of the performance trap (striving for acceptance through good deeds). Receive in prayer and faith God's unconditional love for you.

7. Claim freedom from any stronghold of the enemy. Spirits of unbelief, heaviness, and infirmity commonly attack those who have a rejection complex. Resist those spirits in the name of Jesus! Renew your mind in God's Word; immerse your heart and mind in Scripture. New thought and behavioral patterns will develop as you nurture a growing intimacy with the Lord, filled with His Word and His Spirit.

8. Cultivate trusting relationships with the Lord and with God-fearing believers. As you make yourself vulnerable to others and find them worthy of your trust and love, you will find healing.

Suggested Prayer

"Father, I come to you in the mighty name of Jesus, my Messiah. I forgive those who have hurt and disappointed me (name them). *I forgive those who abused and used me* (name them). *I forgive all who have rejected me in any way* (name them; include family members and authority figures, living and deceased). *I release my hurt and rejection to you, Lord. Please heal the wounds in my heart; heal every area of brokenness in my soul. Heal my mind and emotions. Please release my repressed emotions; I receive them as a gift from you.*

"I resist and renounce every lie about myself and others that I have believed (name them). (e.g., *"I repent for believing that You cannot be trusted... that all men are abusive... for believing that I am a failure and will never succeed in life." "I renounce the lie that I deserve to be rejected."*) *I resist every lying spirit in Jesus' name! I resist and rebuke every spirit of unbelief in the name of Jesus. I confess my unbelief and renounce it. Please forgive me and uproot all traces of unbelief from my spirit and soul.*

"In Jesus' name, I break every promise or childhood oath that has held me captive (name those oaths). *Thank You, Jesus, that You still set captives free. Please set me free from the oaths that have bound me. Give me the grace to walk free of their influence. Thank You for forgiving me. Your blood is stronger than my sin and more powerful than the strength of my rebellion. Please cleanse me from all sin. I receive Your forgiveness by faith.*

Thank You for Your love grace. Please free me from the performance trap. I resist every spirit of accusation and condemnation. "There is NO condemnation for those who are in Christ Jesus" **(Rom. 8:1)**.

"I resist and rebuke every spirit of infirmity and command you to leave me. Every sickness or weakness in my flesh that has come through rejection, you have no more right to stay. I belong to Jesus and am accepted in the Beloved; leave me in Jesus' name! Every spirit of heaviness, I command you to leave me in the name of Jesus. I claim my freedom from every manifestation of the spirit of heaviness: depression, inferiority, insecurity, sadness, jealousy, anger, hopelessness, envy, inadequacy, and fear of failure. Be gone, in the name of the Lord Jesus!

"Jesus, please fill my heart and soul with Your peace and joy, love and patience. Fill me with Your goodness, kindness, gentleness, and faithfulness. Immerse me with Your Holy Spirit. Guide me as I read Your Word every day; help me to appropriate Your truth into my life. Thank You for setting and making me free.

"Please show me who I can safely trust in close relationship. Guide me as I learn to trust people and to show love to others without fearing rejection. Give me divine alignments with solid believers, and network me with those of Your choosing. Thank You, Lord. In Jesus' name, amen."

ELEVEN

The Rebellion Complex

"He who is of a proud heart stirs up strife..." **(Prov. 28:25a)**. *"For rebellion is as the sin of witchcraft, and stubbornness is as iniquity and idolatry..."* **(1 Sam. 15:23a)**.

We have seen how people with passive natures withdraw from conflict; now we will look at how people with aggressive natures lash out at those who hurt or reject them. Their personalities reflect anger, resistance, and rebellion. Their attitude is, *"If you hurt me, you'll regret it!"*

At the foundation of the rebellious complex is pride. The foundational sins of the complexes of rejection and rebellion—unbelief and pride—are both extremely offensive to God. They focus on self, resist God's rule, and give birth to numerous other sins. Both personality complexes develop as a result of messages of rejection, but the temptations based in pride are very different from those based in unbelief. The lists of personality traits, though not conclusive, give us a general idea of the problem behaviors, emotions, and thinking processes associated with each complex.

Evidences of Pride in the Emotions

1. anger, antagonism — Anger almost always begins with hurt; recurrent hurt can cause *continual* anger. A person with a bad temper suffers from unresolved, internal conflicts or from inner wounds. If he gives into anger frequently, he will develop an angry personality where he is angry all of the time—waking up angry and going to bed angry. When anger finds no acceptable outlet, it goes underground, and surfaces in a cycle of control and explosions of emotions. The way one reacts to accumulated hurt and anger is to either become depressed or to erupt in rage at the closest target.

2. arrogance, pride — A proud person looks down on others, makes condescending comments, and is vain and egocentric. The distance he keeps from people results in him being very lonely.

3. significant mood swings — Some people cope with reality through excited emotions and, alternately, deep depression. They cannot deal with life and its stresses calmly and maturely. At the base of severe mood swings is unresolved hurt or conflict. *"Even in laughter the heart may sorrow, and the end of mirth may be grief"* (**Prov. 14:13**). (When the mood swings are extreme, the person may have Bipolar Disorder and require medication and therapy.)

Evidences of Pride in the Mind

1. superiority — Commonly seen in the world of academics and sports, people of high intelligence or superior performance may be condescending toward those whom they consider inferior. This includes racial and national prejudices.

2. rivalry, competition — Hurting people perform for approval and love, fear failure, and find their worth in what others think of them. Defensive, they cannot easily receive criticism because they interpret it as rejection.

3. control — People try to control situations in order to keep the direction of love flowing their way. Those raised in an unsafe environment where they feel insecure and powerless often build walls of protection around their hearts and lives. Victims of abuse monitor their circumstances; they subconsciously think, *"If I can control my environment, nothing unexpected will happen."* They believe no one is watching out for them.

4. inflexibility, stubbornness — Individuals with a rebellion complex are obstinate. They rigidly hold on to their opinions or structures at home, work, or school. They resist change because their identity is in what is familiar to them. Rigid people think in terms of hero or betrayer, failure or success. Abuse survivors are often rigid; they repress feelings and maintain tight boundaries for the sake of safety. They appear steadfast, but are usually just stubborn. Stubbornness is being immovable in self; steadfastness is being immovable in God. Stubbornness is not always a conscious choice; it may result from habit patterns developed over a long period of time.

5. arrogance — When one's identity is rooted in his knowledge, his attitude is, *"I know it all! You can't teach me anything!"* He finds it difficult to compliment the knowledge or expertise of someone else. Being arrogant can lead to arguments and strife. Following a church service where my husband preached, a man walked up to him and said, *"What you shared was good, but of course, I knew it already!"*

6. independence — The proud person does not easily acknowledge his needs or limitations. Believing he is sufficient himself, he needs no one. Because people have failed him in the past, he refuses to depend on them. He fears trusting a person who might let him down.

Evidences of Pride in the Human Spirit

1. deception — Pride opens the door to confusion, and confusion distorts the truth. It causes us to believe lies about others and ourselves, and to be paranoid and irrational with fear. **Obadiah 3a** says, *"The pride of your heart has deceived you..."*

In South Africa, there was a resident in a mental hospital who believed he was Jesus Christ. One day a pastor said to him, *"So, you are Jesus! I've read about you in the Bible."* The man replied, *"Really? What does it say about me?"* The pastor said, *"The Bible says you healed many people. You multiplied bread and fish to feed thousands of people. You walked on water...."* The pastor showed the delusional gentleman numerous places in the gospels about what Jesus did and said. After a while, the mental patient quietly said, *"I'm not really Jesus, am I?"* And the pastor gently replied, *"No, you aren't, but I can introduce you to Him."* And he led him into a saving knowledge of the Messiah, Jesus. Soon after that, the patient exhibited clear thinking and understanding, and was released from the mental hospital.

2. resentment, bitterness — When we do not forgive quickly, we begin to resent those who wounded us. The resentment festers into bitterness, and once bitterness takes root, it overwhelms our hearts and contaminates our souls. It will cause us to be harsh, easily offended, and judgmental.

3. criticalness — A critical person is negative and judgmental. Short on mercy and grace, he is difficult to please and indifferent to the needs of others. He sets high standards, often far above what is reasonable. When he does not meet his standards, he feels a sense of failure, frustration, and despondency. When he *does* meet them, he is proud of himself and critical of those who live beneath his criterion.

Sam was over 30 and still subconsciously hoping to win his father's approval. His father was a perfectionist, and Sam never felt he had met his standards. As a result, Sam felt inadequate and had low self-esteem. His romantic relationships were always of short duration, and he was unsuccessful in work. Because he didn't seem to be good enough for his father, he quit trying. He felt rejected by his one whose opinion of him mattered the most – his Dad. Although his mother expressed her love to him, he was unable to make a success of his life.

4. possessiveness — Being possessive is a normal reaction to fears of rejection, abuse, or abandonment. We are possessive when we try to live one's life for him, dictating whom he can see and what he can do.

5. manipulation — Controlling through deceptive or indirect means is called manipulation. *Indifferent* manipulators do not acknowledge how they really feel to others; they deny their feelings. Being shut down emotionally or passively aggressive, they seldom communicate on anything but a surface level. This form of manipulation destroys relationships. *Active* manipulators seek to maintain control at all costs. They are dominant in most of their relationships. *Passive* manipulators appear helpless and needy. They attempt to win by losing and may cry or whine to get their way. Passive manipulators are typically women. *Competitive* manipulators use both passive and active manipulation.

Little Tom asked his big brother for the ball. Unsuccessful, he then *cried* for the ball to be given to him. When that failed, he *demanded* the ball! He had moved from passive to active manipulation.

The final end of the rebellion complex is homicide. It is venting wrath on another to the point of murder.

Distinctive Behaviors of Rebellion

1. unrestrained living — Rebellious people live as if God does not exist. Rebelling against His authority, they become their own authority, enslaved to themselves. The areas they control, the devil will attempt to take over. Slavery to bodily appetites results in immorality, obesity, alcoholism, or drug addiction. Slavery to emotions can result in rage, depression, paranoia, or panic. Slavery to the intellect may result in rationalism or intellectualism.

Any place where we harden our hearts to the control of the Holy Spirit, we move into sin. **Proverbs 28:14** says, *"Happy is the man who is always reverent, but he who hardens his heart will fall into calamity."*

2. surface relationship with God — They try to relate to the Lord on the basis of their accomplishments rather than through the blood of Jesus. Their lives may be filled with good deeds, but they have no intimate relationship with God.

Both those who are guilty of unbelief and those who are proud have a poor relationship with the Lord. The unbelieving work hard to please God, but they don't feel they can no matter how hard they try. The proud work hard to please God and believe they do! But God's Word says our relationship with God is not established on the basis of our works, but on the basis of His grace. *"Not by works of righteousness which we have done, but according to His mercy He saved us, through the washing of regeneration and renewing of the Holy Spirit"* **(Tit. 3:5)**.

3. attempt to assume God's role — The proud enter into enemy territory, often into witchcraft. Witchcraft is outright rebellion against God. It is not just casting spells, placing curses, and using black magic; it is any time we assume God's role. In **Isaiah 14:14**, Lucifer (Satan) says, *"I will be like the Most High."* He is the epitome of rebellion.

There are three areas where we can unknowingly enter Satan's territory: (1) when we usurp Jesus' Lordship over others through manipulation or control, (2) when we seek revenge (**Romans 12:19** says, *"Beloved, do not avenge yourselves, but rather give place to wrath; for it is written, 'Vengeance is Mine, I will repay,' says the Lord."*), and (3) when we covet supernatural power. All power belongs to God, so when we covet supernatural power, we can easily enter into the enemy's domain.

Action to Take

Look back over the evidences of rebellion. Ask the Holy Spirit to show you where you are proud. Repent of and renounce any sin you see reflected in your emotions, mind, or spirit. Then look at the behaviors of the rebellion complex. Pray through them, repenting where necessary.

Ask the Lord to whom you can confess your sin and who will hold you accountable as you seek freedom and healing. We all need people to journey with us, helping us to put off the old man and put on the new. Don't be afraid or ashamed to ask someone to listen to and pray with you. *"Confess your trespasses to one another, and pray for one another, that you may be healed. The effective, fervent prayer of a righteous man avails much"* (**Jam. 5:16**).

For more help in finding deliverance from rebellion, read and pray through the next chapter.

TWELVE

Freedom from Rebellion

"Prepare the way of the Lord; make straight in the desert a highway for our God. Every...mountain and hill [shall be] *brought low... The glory of the Lord shall be revealed..."* **(Isa. 40:3b-4a, 5a)**. *"A man's pride will bring him low, but the humble in spirit will retain honor"* **(Prov. 29:23)**.

To be carriers of God's glory, we need to bring down every high place of personal pride, breaking its stronghold over us. Pride specializes in self-seeking, self-will, and self-confidence. It is the strengthening of that which cannot enter nor possess the things of God's kingdom. Pride refuses to let Jesus be king; it enthrones self.

Proud people seek revenge when hurt. They protect themselves and attack anyone who threatens their position. Their aggressive behavior is revealed by hostility, anger, and competitiveness. In **John 5:44**, Jesus said, *"How can you believe, who receive honor one from another, and do not seek the honor that comes from the only God?"* In other words, how can you have faith in God and depend on Him when you are looking for recognition and honor from one another? Pride inspires you to seek personal glory and neutralizes faith.

Do you have a problem with pride? To find out, ask yourself these questions:

1. When someone is given a position you wanted, or if one's gifts, talents, or accomplishments surpass yours, are you jealous or angry?

2. How do you react when someone gives you constructive criticism in love? Does it make you defensive or resentful?

3. Do you want people to notice, affirm, and appreciate you? Are you hurt when you are overlooked or insulted?

Rooting Out Pride

Pride begins the same way unbelief does—from messages of rejection. To uproot pride from our lives, we need to do more than merely repent. We also need to forgive those who caused our pain or rejected us, and surrender all hurt and anger to the Lord. We need to ask for and receive the Lord's forgiveness for withholding forgiveness from others.

We must repent of pride and its evidences in our emotions, mind, and spirit. We also need to confess and renounce any behavioral patterns of pride. When our life motivation is love for God, we will be able to confess our faults to someone we trust. Confessing to a person roots sin out deeply; it makes us accountable to someone. Humility protects us from being as susceptible to that same sin in the future. *"Confess your trespasses* [faults] *to one another, and pray for one another that you may be healed"* (**Jam. 5:16a**).

To root out pride, we must walk in the opposite spirit of humility. Humility is realizing that we do not know it all and that our way is not always right. It is being flexible and teachable. In humility, we pursue transparency and openness in relationships; we avoid hypocrisy and independence. We live in the light and are willing to be known despite the consequences. We are genuine no matter what others may think.

How humble are you? Are you broken before God and open about your failures and need of mercy? Do you thank God for His love and grace, and honor Him in thought, word, and deed? Do you seek God's glory rather than your own? Do you look for the best in others and pray for their weaknesses, refusing to gossip or criticize? Do you hate sin, determined not to give the enemy any opportunity to rejoice over you? Do you forgive quickly and walk in peace? Do you fear God more than man?

As we prepare for Jesus' return, we need to topple every mountain of pride in our lives. Let's prepare a highway for our God to stride down victoriously so that His glory is revealed in us! *"Arise, shine; for your light has come! And the glory of the Lord is risen upon you...the Lord will arise over you, and His glory will be seen upon you"* (**Isa. 60:1-2**).

THIRTEEN

Knowing Father's Love

"And we have seen and testify that the Father has sent the Son as Savior of the world. Whoever confesses that Jesus is the Son of God, God abides in him, and he in God. And we have known and believed the love that God has for us. God is love, and he who abides in love abides in God, and God in him" (**1 John 4:14-16**).

A little girl walked to and from her school every day. The weather one morning indicated an approaching storm. By afternoon, the wind was strong and lightning flashed. The girl's mother thought her daughter might be frightened as she walked home, and she feared the electrical storm might harm her. Concerned, she quickly got into her car and raced toward the school. Soon, she saw her little girl walking along. At each flash of lightning, the child would stop, look up, and smile. As she drew up beside her daughter, she lowered the window of the car and asked, *"What are you doing?"* The girl answered, *"I am trying to look pretty because God keeps taking my picture!"*

Perception is Critical

Theologian and author A. W. Tozer wrote, *"What comes into your mind when you think about God is the most important thing about you."* Our concept of God influences every area of our lives. It determines how we relate to ourselves, to others, and to the situations we encounter. Everything that defines us is influenced by our perception of Him.

Why is it possible to hold a wrong image of God in our hearts despite the clear teachings of Scripture about Him? It is because the negative things we learn and experience in our early relationships with those close to us are so deep and powerful that they reduce the teaching of Scripture to mere head knowledge.

To uncover the roots of how we perceive God, it is important to look at our relationships with our parents or guardians. We who have healthy relationships with our fathers or male guardians usually relate positively to God as Father. However, we who struggle with and are disappointed in our primary relationships often find connecting with God difficult.

Our faulty views of God can cause us to fear intimacy with Him. They inspire us to labor for Him out of duty or fear rather than out of love. If we see God as a loving Father, we will draw near to Him; if He seems to be a harsh judge, we will withdraw from Him. If we do not believe God cares about us, we will be overly focused on caring for ourselves. If we feel insignificant or ignored by Him, we will weary ourselves seeking significance from people.

Distorted images of God affect how we worship Him. We may question if He is worthy of our worship. Our witness will also be affected; the more we admire and love Him, the more we want others to know Him like we do. We can rise no higher in our spiritual life than our view or concept of God.

Many people judge God to be unapproachable, passive, hard to please, or angry. They expect Him to be just like their earthly fathers or guardians. But God is perfect and wonderful; He is sovereign, loving, and wise. We cannot press the Creator of the universe into the finite shape of a man.

In the earthly realm, it is the father that gives his child self-worth, value, security, and an identity as masculine or feminine. He is largely responsible for the child's self-image. The same is true in the spiritual realm: the Heavenly Father gives us value, worth, and security. He gives us our identity as His children. He shows us who we are through Scripture. It is through an intimate relationship with Him that we are made whole. Even if our parents (or significant others) have failed us, we can be restored in our souls through knowing the love of the Father. What we missed in our important primary relationships, God can provide.

Jesus came to earth to reveal His Father to us and to redeem us, reconciling us to God. We attain salvation through Jesus, and we find our worth and security in knowing the Father's love. Once we meet Jesus at salvation, we need to develop an intimate relationship with the Father. He is our ultimate destination!

Most of us need some degree of healing in our souls to correct our distortions of God's Fatherhood and to mend the wounds of the past. We need a revelation of the Father's love! It is through the blood of Jesus that we come into salvation, and it is through the love of the Father that we find wholeness.

Steps toward Healing

1. We separate our concept of God from our concept of authority figures. In the areas where our guardians failed us, we expect God to fail us also. In our hearts, we judge them as inadequate, and we transfer that judgment onto God. We expect to receive from God the same injustices we received from them. In our minds, we put on Him their limitations and personality traits. We perceive God through glasses colored by the mannerisms of our guardians.

We need to see God as He really is, not as we perceive Him to be according to our education, culture, early experiences, and representation by authorities. We must accept what the Bible says about God as being absolutely true—that He is wise, loving, and almighty.

Jesus showed us what His Father is like while He was on earth. In **John 14:9b-10**, Jesus said, *"...He who has seen Me has seen the Father; so how can you say, 'Show us the Father?' Do you not believe that I am in the Father and the Father in Me? The words that I speak to you I do not speak on My own authority; but the Father who dwells in Me does the works."*

2. We forgive those who hurt us. When we forgive our parents and/or other authorities, we also release the anger, hurt, or sense of injustice. As we forgive, we cancel the debt we feel they owe us. We entrust them to God, refusing to hold animosity against them.

We must also ask God to forgive us for judging Him wrongly. We must embrace the truth of Who God is as revealed in His Word.

3. We repent of our wrong reactions to hurt. While needing God's love to heal the wounds we sustained from authorities, we also need to repent of our reactions to that pain—what we have become as a result of them. Most people become bitter, fearful, and angry because of inner wounds. **Psalm 41:4** says, *"...Lord, be merciful to me; heal my soul, for I have sinned against You."* **Isaiah 59:2** says, *"...your iniquities have separated you from your God; and your sins have hidden His face from you."* We need to repent of our sin and receive God's forgiveness.

4. We receive God's love. When we face our past pain, we realize how desperately we need to believe in God's unconditional love. Human love alone cannot heal us. We need God's love, which far outweighs the hurts in our inner man. We have all been wounded; we all have a love deficit that only His love can fill. We must *believe* in our hearts that God loves us unconditionally, as well as know it in our minds. If we welcome His love deep into our souls, it can set us free and heal us from the power of hurtful words or wounds.

If we only focus on God's mercy and love, we cheapen His grace. We also need to realize that He is holy and requires us to be holy. *"... we have had human fathers who corrected us, and we paid them respect. Shall we not much more readily be in subjection to the Father of spirits and live? For they indeed for a few days chastened us as seemed best to them, but He for our profit, that we may be partakers of His holiness"* (**Heb. 12:9-10**).

We must perceive the Lord as He actually is, with the proper balance of mercy and truth, grace and justice. When we worship God as the holy, just and merciful One, we will find that we become more whole and holy ourselves. We become like that which we worship.

5. We let God parent us. We feel secure in knowing we are loved and cherished by God. **Psalm 27:10** says, *"When my mother and my father forsake me, then the Lord will take care of me."*

The Lord can give us what our parents failed to give us. As a good Father, He is committed to us, loves us unconditionally, disciplines and blesses us, and affirms us by giving us His undivided attention.

Psalm 27:11 says, *"Teach me Your way, O Lord..."* In Hebrew, David begins the prayer with *"Horeni."* Another form of this word "to teach," comes from the Hebrew root *horim*, which means "parents." David was asking God to teach him as a parent. Parents are responsible to teach their children the ways of God, but too often they fail. David experienced that, so he cried to the Lord, *"Teach me as a parent"* or *"Parent me!" "Behold what manner of love the Father has bestowed on us, that we should be called children of God..."* (**1 John 3:1a**). The Father's love transmits value and safety to us.

6. We cultivate our intimacy with God as Father. As we grow in our experience with and knowledge of God, we are secured in His love and the pains of rejection will heal. We must choose to believe that everything God says in His Word is absolutely true, and counter the lies we formerly believed with the Scriptures. **Isaiah 43:4a** speaks of His love for us: *"Since you were precious in My sight, you have been honored, and I have loved you..."*

Suggested Prayer

"Father, thank You for loving me. When I look at the cross, I believe that You love me as much as You say You do! I forgive all those who misrepresented You to me. I forgive them for the disappointment and pain they caused me. I confess my sin of judging authorities; please forgive me. I'm sorry for the ways I reacted selfishly in my hurt and anger. I release my expectations of others to you, and I place all my hope and expectations on You. Please parent me! Give me Your parental blessing of affirmation, commitment, discipline, and unconditional love. I repent for believing lies about You and for judging and accusing You. Forgive me and cleanse me from these sins. Give me a revelation of Who You are, especially as my Father. Fill the empty places in my heart with Your love. Heal the wounds in my soul. Help me grow in my relationship with You; I want to know You intimately. In Jesus' name, amen."

FOURTEEN

Repentance – the First Step Toward Freedom

"The Lord is not slack concerning His promise, as some count slackness, but is longsuffering toward us, not willing that any should perish but that all should come to repentance" (**2 Pet. 3:9**). *"Or do you despise the riches of His goodness, forbearance, and longsuffering, not knowing that the goodness of God leads you to repentance?"* (**Rom. 2:4**).

In **Matthew 4:17**, Jesus began His ministry preaching, *"Repent: for the kingdom of heaven is at hand."* Jesus did not draw the crowds by inviting the sick to receive healing or by raising the dead. He began His public ministry by stressing the need for repentance toward God. He knew that miracles would produce only temporal awareness of God's kingdom and not the lasting fruit that repentance would bring. Jesus did not want His listeners to only be *aware* of the kingdom; He wanted them to be *a part* of it! He wanted them *in* His kingdom, experiencing His joy, peace, and righteousness.

To repent is to think differently, to change one's mind and direction. It is to turn from self-rule to Jesus' Lordship, from going one's own way to going God's way. The Bible does not preach salvation apart from repentance. Calling on the name of the Lord Jesus and surrendering the management of our lives to Him results in our salvation.

St. Gregory the Great said, *"God never intended a distinction between being a Christian and being a disciple."* Many people call themselves believers today, but their lives are not like the Messiah's at all. They live more for themselves than for Jesus. But God has a higher plan for us; He wants us to become like His Son in all areas of character, conduct, and power-filled ministry. We are not called to be partially like Jesus; we are to be *fully* transformed into His image (see **Rom. 8:29**). Being Jesus' disciple means we make Him central in our lives where all that we do revolves around Him. It is like signing a blank check to God and saying, *"Here, Lord, fill it in. I delight to do Your will."*

"In those days John the Baptist came preaching in the wilderness of Judea, and saying, 'Repent, for the kingdom of heaven is at hand!' For this is he who was spoken of by the prophet Isaiah, saying: 'The voice of one crying in the wilderness: "Prepare the way of the Lord; make His paths straight." '...Then Jerusalem, all Judea, and all the region around the Jordan went out to him and were baptized by him in the Jordan, confessing their sins. But when he saw many of the Pharisees and Sadducees coming to his baptism, he said to them, 'Brood of vipers! Who warned you to flee from the wrath to come? Therefore bear fruits worthy of repentance' " (**Matt. 3:1-3, 5-8**).

Repentance is Basic to Christianity

To invite the Lord into our lives without repenting would be like saying, "Jesus, come into my life. Don't mind all the stuff I have around; just climb over it, walk around it, and duck your head to miss the low-hanging objects. I want to go to heaven, but I want my junk too, so come on in—my way."

In Luke 4:5-8, we read that the devil offered Jesus a way to receive kingdoms, authority, and glory without going to the cross. But Jesus refused, knowing that redemption could not be purchased if He were not crucified. The devil offers us the same shortcut. He says we can have God's kingdom and authority and share in His glory without sacrifice. He offers us a *cross-less* Christianity. But the cross is the entryway into God's kingdom! The cross always confronts the flesh, so embracing it will affect every area of our lives.

The apostle Paul spoke of repentance before saving faith when he wrote, *"testifying to Jews, and also to Greeks, repentance toward God and faith toward our Lord Jesus Christ"* (**Acts 20:21**).

When Jesus was giving His farewell speech to His men in Luke 24, He told them to preach repentance first and remission of sins second. He said, *"...it was necessary for the Messiah to suffer and to rise from the dead the third day, and that repentance and remission of sins should be preached in His name to all nations..."* (**Luke 24:46b-47a**).

Only when we repent can we become candidates for the grace of God. We repent of sin in word by confession and in action by a change of lifestyle and restitution. The fruit of repentance is evidenced in our actions, attitudes, motives, thoughts, values, and words. When we have surrendered our lives to King Jesus, we don't live like we used to. We don't speak as we once did. We ask Jesus to reign in our lives, and to manifest His righteousness in and through us. We choose to crucify the flesh and live for God. We resolve to demonstrate God's love through blessing instead of criticizing, giving instead of hoarding, and listening attentively instead of talking too much.

Once the Holy Spirit convicts us of sin, we confess it to God, naming it what He names it. (If it's lust, we call it lust, not just desire and interest.) We ask God to forgive us and to cleanse us from all unrighteousness (**1 John 1:9**). When possible, confess your sin to the one who was hurt by it and make restitution: return what you took; pay what you owe. Renounce any foundational sins (i.e., pride and unbelief) that invite further sin and carnality. Thank God for His salvation and mercy toward you.

Suggested Prayer

"Father God, I come to You in the name of Jesus Christ. Thank You for sending Jesus to pay the price for my redemption. Thank You, Jesus, for offering Yourself as a sacrifice for my sin. I feel convicted of __________ and confess this to You as sin. I choose to turn from it and to live righteously. Please forgive me and uproot this sin from my life. Deliver me and cleanse me from all unrighteousness! I receive Your forgiveness by faith; please show me if I should confess this sin to anyone else. Thank You, Lord."

Repenting of Sexual Misconduct

"Flee sexual immorality. Every sin that a man does is outside the body, but he who commits sexual immorality sins against his own body" (**1 Cor. 6:18**). Sexual sin damages our souls more than other sins do. People guilty of moral sin find it harder to release guilt and shame, and to receive forgiveness than do those who sin in other areas.

When they repent of the sexual activity, they should also repent of sins connected to that particular sin. Below are lists that will guide you or the one you are counseling into more thorough repentance. If there are other sexual sins to confess, you can use these lists, adapting them as needed.

When repenting of ADULTERY, also repent of:

1. inflicting pain on others
2. stealing one's spouse, his/her happiness, and breaking up the home
3. causing the children pain and shame
4. telling lies and being deceitful
5. disobeying God and bringing disgrace on Him and His people
6. abusing your body which is His temple (*see* **1 Cor. 6:19-20**)

When repenting of FORNICATION, also repent of:

1. provoking another to sin against his or her conscience
2. using another for your pleasure and self-gratification
3. encouraging (perhaps unintentionally) the other person to further sexual misbehavior
4. causing a pregnancy
5. putting a stigma on the illegitimate child (or abortion/murder)
6. being disobedient to God

When repenting of HOMOSEXUALITY, also repent of:

1. sinning against God and indulging the flesh
2. dishonoring and abusing your body
3. involving others and passing on the perversion
4. shaming the family
5. being dishonest and deceitful in covering the sin
6. rejecting yourself and/or your gender
7. blaming God "for making you this way" (This is a lie.)

We need to make a clean break from all wrong relationships and flee from temptation. We need to surrender all situations to Jesus and not merely ask for His help.

If we only ask for help, we are still in control. We must throw themselves on God's mercy and His ability to save us.

An Integrated Approach to Freedom is Best

Repentance is a big part of one's healing, but it is not the whole picture. The roots of sin must be discovered and dealt with, forgiveness received and extended, inner wounds prayed for, and demonic influences removed through deliverance. Praying into generational influences and iniquity are often part of the healing package. An integrated approach to freedom secures the best and most lasting results.

May the Lord guide you as you continue on your pathway to freedom, and anoint you as you bring those enslaved to sin out of captivity into liberty.

"Stand fast therefore in the liberty by which Christ has made us free, and do not be entangled again with a yoke of bondage...walk in the Spirit, and you shall not fulfill the lust of the flesh" (**Gal. 5:1, 16**).

FIFTEEN

Freedom from Guilt

"...O my God, I am too ashamed and humiliated to lift up my face to You, my God; for our iniquities have risen higher than our heads, and our guilt has grown up to the heavens. Since the days of our fathers to this day we have been very guilty, and for our iniquities we, our kings, and our priests have been delivered into the hand of the kings of the lands, to the sword, to captivity, to plunder, and to humiliation, as it is this day" (**Ezra 9:6-7**).

Guilt is the awareness and regret of having committed an offense. It is the feeling of responsibility for having done something that violated a personal moral standard, or the mental and emotional pain we experience when we have neglected to do something right. Any time we fall short of God's standards, our consciences are defiled and guilt is produced. If we cover that guilt without dealing with it directly with the blood of Jesus, it will affect us emotionally. This is especially true for moral transgressions; they defile the conscience more than other sins. Moral sins must be confessed and forgiven *specifically* for the feelings of guilt to be removed.

We may try to ease guilt by punishing ourselves (often unconsciously) through overwork, sickness, isolation from others, or physical pain. The law of self-atonement says if we punish ourselves, we can feel better about our guilt. Sometimes we deal with guilt by projecting it onto others. We make our problems their fault. This is often seen in stressed marriages.

Guilt can cause emotional responses such as nervousness, depression, lack of concentration, anger, excessive self-consciousness, and low self-esteem. We may be able to see the faults of others but be blind to our own. Our hearts harden when we refuse to deal with guilt. It causes us to doubt our relationship with God. Because we feel we cannot please Him, we feel insecure with Him.

Those who live with a guilty conscience are usually hypocritical, anxious, and fearful. They occasionally develop mental illnesses. They fear intimacy, knowing that if someone knows them well, they will discover the cause of their guilt.

Basic Truths

1. Guilt is a reality. We feel guilty because we *are* guilty. **James 2:10** says, *"For whoever shall keep the whole law, and yet stumble in one point, he is guilty of all."* Conviction of sin is a belief about our actions, not just a feeling of being good or bad.

2. God does not want us to remain under the curse of guilt. Jesus paid the penalty for us so that we can be free. **John 8:34b-36** says, *"...whoever commits sin is a slave of sin. And a slave does not abide in the house forever, but a son abides forever. Therefore if the Son makes you free, you shall be free indeed."*

3. Humans tend toward evil and think about it easily. It is just as wrong to ponder sin after it has been forgiven, as it is to imagine it and plan it. When we condemn ourselves for pardoned sin, we waste time and emotional energy punishing ourselves over actions for which God has already cleansed us. We can quench the Spirit by reliving old sins just as we can by committing new ones.

Guilt-ridden people have trouble fixing their eyes on Jesus. Helping people look at Jesus and not at their sin is one of the most productive ways we can help them work through guilt. *"...since we are surrounded by so great a cloud of witnesses, let us lay aside every weight, and the sin which so easily ensnares us, and let us run with endurance the race that is set before us, looking unto Jesus, the author and finisher of our faith..."* (**Heb. 12:1-2a**).

4. Feelings of guilt must be evaluated in terms of God's Word. Guilt is only a virtue if it leads to remorse, repentance, and an abiding relationship with Jesus. Because guilt keeps us from intimacy with God (something He greatly desires), He offers forgiveness to all who repent. He responds with wrath only where there is no repentance.

Isaiah 53:4-6 explains how Jesus' death satisfied God's righteous judgment for sin and provides healing for our sin nature. From a legal standpoint, God forgives mankind on the basis of the debt having been paid. We must not feel guilty for sin that we have confessed because our debt was paid in full with the blood of Jesus. If we hold onto guilt after confessing our sin to the Lord, we are saying that Jesus' blood is insufficient for it. We are calling His blood common, trampling the Son of God underfoot, and insulting the Spirit of grace (*see* **Heb. 10:29**).

Challenges of Counseling Guilt Issues

People who struggle with guilt and receiving forgiveness are difficult to help. Some of the common challenges of counseling them are:

1. communicating understanding — Most people suffer guilt in silence. They believe that if their sin were known, they would be rejected. As counselors, we communicate acceptance by carefully listening. Then, we determine if they are dealing with real guilt or condemnation (false guilt). Guilty feelings may come from a variety of sources other than sin, such as: unfulfilled expectations they have had or that loved ones have for them.

2. helping counselees find peace — To move beyond guilt, counselees must receive forgiveness and forgive others. They may need healing for damaged emotions and for destructive patterns of thinking and believing.

3. avoiding quick solutions — Most quick answers *("Just believe God forgives you!")* can leave the hurting person feeling worse. When you give scriptural answers to someone regarding guilt, explain practically how the person is to appropriate those verses.

4. realizing there may be multiple problems — Other sins or problems may accompany guilt, such as anger, depression, physical complaints, substance abuse, or social inadequacies. Once a person has dealt with the guilt, he then may need to deal with the habits that he has formed because of it. He may need an accountability partner and/or guidance in finding lasting freedom.

A young lady went for prayer and counsel regarding the satanic ritual abuse she had suffered at the hands of her father, a satanic high priest. She realized she had to forgive her father and then repent for her own willing involvement in the occult. Following that, she had to learn appropriate social skills and to overcome an eating disorder. Dealing with the guilt wasn't her only problem; she had to overcome other issues, too.

King David struggled with guilt over his sins. He had tremendous regret and repented deeply, as we see in Psalm 51. After he confessed his sin, David found a new place of fellowship with God. He learned the key to moving forward after sin threatened to destroy him, and revealed that key in **Psalm 32:5**: *"I acknowledged my sin to You, and my iniquity I have not hidden. I said, 'I will confess my transgressions to the Lord,' and You forgave the iniquity of my sin."* God removed David's guilt and forgave him. He did NOT say to David, *"I'll forgive you, but I'll never trust you again."* No, He restored him.

God restores people today, too. However, the trust of *others* may need to be earned. If the failure was in an area of fidelity, the guilty person will need to earn trust again by proving his faithfulness. As counselors, we must be able to address sin without destroying the person or our relationship with him. When Jesus spoke to the woman at the well in John 4, He asked questions that enabled her to confess her sin. He led her to discover her need of salvation, but He did not attack her with condemnation.

When you see signs of guilt in counselees, you can ask questions that enable them to confess their sin, such as:

- Are you at peace with God, with yourself, and with others?
- Have you dealt with all guilt—past and present?
- Do you have a clean conscience before God?

Distinguish between True and False Guilt

True guilt is the set of thoughts and feelings that usually accompany sinful behavior. A person *feels* guilty because he *is* guilty.

A law has been broken or a person has been hurt. Unearned (false) guilt is often tied to perfectionist standards. It is usually related to what we have *not* done. Key words to notice are "I should have…" and "if only…" (e.g. *"If only I hadn't left him alone..."*)

Ask questions to determine if the guilt is true or false:

- Can you say what you have done is sinful or wrong?
- If you had to ask forgiveness for something, what would it be?
- If you asked forgiveness of someone, who would it be?

If the person cannot come up with clear answers to any of these questions, he is probably dealing with false guilt. In that case, you might ask one or more of these questions:

- What expectations do you have for yourself that you haven't met?
- Who are the people you feel you have disappointed?
- Are you putting demands on yourself that you can't live up to?
- Have you disappointed yourself?

In most cases, people with false guilt need to deal with the impossibilities of their perfectionist thinking and throw off unrealistic expectations others have placed on them.

The Role of Love in Healing

Receiving love from others is healing to people who struggle with unearned guilt and/or shame. Since it is beneficial for people to talk through their feelings (it helps reveal possible distortions), the most loving thing to do for guilt-ridden people is to ask them questions that will help them understand themselves and their feelings. The least loving approach is to tell them how they "should" feel. Patient love says, *"I have time for you. I will be with you as you sort out your life. Tell me more. I value you as a person."*

It is difficult for those who have only known conditional love to receive God's unconditional love and forgiveness. Counselees frequently fear that God's love has requirements that they cannot meet. They may say they believe in His love, but not feel it. It is important that they see God as His Word reveals Him to be—loving, merciful, and just—as they will relate to God as they perceive Him.

One of our roles as counselors is to help people understand that God's love for them is unconditional. You might ask, *"What if God is able to love you unconditionally? What if He has forgiven your sin already and you can go forward without guilt? If God were to love you without conditions, how would you act differently? What kind of choices would you make?"* You could suggest to a counselee that he go through an entire day believing God loves him as much as He says He does. Sometimes living the truth is necessary to shape one's ability to believe it.

It is important that we don't just tell people what to do; we also need to tell them *how* to do those things. We must give them instruction and practical steps to take, and guide them step-by-step toward confession, forgiveness, and proper behavior. Asking for forgiveness and forgiving others may seem simple, but it can involve fear and emotional blocks that a counselee may not understand. Support him as he attempts to take the steps of action you suggest.

Take care not to condemn people for their failures. We all make mistakes! We are rightly related to God *only* because of what Jesus has done for us. *"...Christ is the end of the law for righteousness to everyone who believes"* (**Rom. 10:4**).

Preventing Further Guilt

Guilt can confuse and immobilize. Encourage proper action by asking, *"What do you feel you need to do to get things going the direction you think they should go?"* If the counselee cannot answer this question, it shows he may not know the source of his guilt. Hold people accountable to make proper choices and to follow through with them.

It is God's love and grace that holds us steady in temptation. We are not to appeal to fear and guilt to keep people from sinning, but to a love relationship with Jesus and an appropriation of His grace.

Help counselees leave the past behind. Ask them if they have requested God's forgiveness and made restitution with man. Encourage them to receive God's forgiveness despite their feelings. Feelings are real, but are not always true. Remind them of 1 John 1:9. Help them line up their thinking with the Word of God, not with their feelings or fears. Talk through their guilt and fears with them, and help them straighten out their distorted ideas and to release unfulfilled expectations.

Sin and guilt are overcome by mercy and salvation. The effective way to deal with guilt is to bring it to the cross, repent of the sin, confess it, and receive God's forgiveness. The blood of Jesus is stronger and more powerful than any sin! *"There is therefore now no condemnation to those who are in Christ Jesus, who do not walk according to the flesh but according to the Spirit"* (**Rom. 8:1**).

Hear Jesus say something like this to you: *"Don't berate yourself over past sin. I suffered and died for all of your sins, including the one you are worried about now. Receive My gift of forgiveness. When you despise yourself for your sins, you are insulting My death on the cross and My resurrection, and declaring that the power of your sin is greater than My power to cleanse and forgive! Let those negative feelings go as your receive My mercy and forgiveness."*

SIXTEEN

A Clear Conscience

"Examine me, O Lord, and prove me; try my mind and my heart" (**Ps. 26:2**). *"...the purpose of the commandment is love from a pure heart, from a good conscience, and from sincere faith"* (**1 Tim. 1:5**).

To have peace with ourselves, we must first have peace with God. If we are not at peace with Him *or* ourselves, we cannot be at peace with anyone else. When we feel estranged from God, we can easily feel threatened and become defensive. We experience turmoil within and may express irritation, anger, or jealousy.

A lack of peace indicates a sense of guilt, and residues of guilt and shame reveal a defiled conscience. Remember the line of the well-known hymn, *"He breaks the power of cancelled sin..."?* The hymnist was referring to sin that is cancelled and yet has power over us due to guilt or inner pain. The antidote is a cleansed conscience.

Sincere faith follows a good conscience. You cannot walk by faith if you do not have a clear conscience. **1 John 3:21** supports this truth: *"Beloved, if our heart does not condemn us, we have confidence toward God."* When our hearts accuse us, we have trouble believing and receiving God's promises by faith. If the devil can rob you of a clear conscience, he can steal your confidence toward God.

1 John 1:8-9 says if we deny that we have sinned or excuse or justify our wrong attitudes, words, or actions, we deceive ourselves. But if we will humble ourselves and confess our sin to God, He will forgive us and cleanse us from all unrighteousness.

Your conscience suffers if you react or defend yourself when treated harshly. Receive God's peace and respond with forgiveness and kindness, if for no other reason than to maintain a pure conscience before God. If you do good and suffer for it, God comes to your defense. Which do you want more—to be treated right by God or by man?

"For this is commendable, if because of conscience toward God one endures grief, suffering wrongfully. For what credit is it if, when you are beaten for your faults, you take it patiently? But when you do good and suffer, if you take it patiently, this is commendable before God" **(1 Pet. 2:19-20)**.

Two things purge a person's conscience: the blood of Jesus (*see* **Heb. 9:13-14**) and honest, honorable living (*see* **Heb. 13:18**). We need both! We must apply Jesus' blood to our conscience, asking Him to wash it with His blood, and we must choose to live honorably from now on.

Suggested Prayer

"Lord Jesus, thank You for shedding Your blood to atone for my sin. I receive Your salvation and forgiveness. Forgive me for defending myself when I've been treated harshly and for reacting to situations wrongly. Teach me how to endure injustices and to suffer patiently. Cleanse my conscience from dead works, sin, and guilt. Wash it with Your blood. I resist all condemnation in Jesus' name. Thank You for the gift of a clear conscience. Lord, by Your grace I choose to live honorably from this day forward. Help me, O Lord, I pray, amen."

SEVENTEEN

Freedom from Iniquity

"His own iniquities entrap the wicked man and he is caught in the cords of his sin. He shall die for lack for instruction and in the greatness of his folly he shall go astray" **(Prov. 5:22-23)**. *"...Let* everyone *who names the name of Christ depart from iniquity"* **(2 Tim. 2:19c)**. *"For Your name's sake, O Lord, pardon my iniquity, for it is great"* **(Ps. 25:11)**.

What Is Iniquity?

The Hebrew word *avon* means iniquity, evil, fault, sin, guilt, blame, moral illness, perversion, crookedness, and punishment of iniquity. *Avon* is derived from the root word *avah*, which means to bend, make crooked, distort, or pervert. Iniquity is more than sin or transgression. It is an evil bent—a propensity to engage in particular sins inherited from forefathers. The sinful tendencies that we are born with will direct the course of our lives if they are not removed.

Iniquity and DNA

Scientists tell us that if each organ in our bodies is broken down to the least common denominator, all cells will be similar; they contain the same DNA as that of the whole person. If a person's DNA strand is untwisted, it can be played as a melody on a piano because of its vibrations. Through the trauma of sin, one's "song" can be changed from a major key to a minor key by the simple altering of the frequency. The DNA is altered by negative attachments to the strand through one's personal sin or generational iniquity.

King David said, *"Behold, I was brought forth in iniquity and in sin my mother conceived me"* **(Ps. 51:5)**. All humans are born with iniquity attached to their DNA. We are conceived in sin; it is inherent in our humanity. Particular sin tendencies and evil inclinations are inherited from our fathers and forefathers, and with each succeeding generation, they become stronger and more controlling. Wickedness begets greater wickedness.

An iniquitous pattern can affect your entire physical and mental makeup because the life is in the blood, which contains DNA. Blood cells are pumped through the body, giving oxygen to each organ. DNA molecules give hereditary instructions. If a message is passed on that has been "twisted" (linked with iniquity), those erroneous instructions leave an impact. Iniquity causes scarring within or on the strands of DNA.

Scientists from Great Britain did a study on genetic scarring. They took a group of individuals and reviewed their lives. They examined what they called their "poor lifestyle choices" (gambling, a sexual perversion, major theft), and found, upon viewing their DNA, that scarred strands appeared in the exact spot on their DNA strands that corresponded to the time and the lifestyle choice that was made.

While one person may be predisposed toward addictions and gambling, another may be predisposed toward stealing and adultery. Although we are all born in sin and conceived in iniquity, we are susceptible to specific temptations according to our patterns of iniquity and the environments in which we were raised.

Some Christian leaders believe that iniquity is the principle cause of sickness, saying that iniquity begins in the spirit of man, travels through the soul, and results in a destructive manifestation in the body. Some psychosomatic diseases may be more than just chemical reactions caused by thoughts and feelings; they may result from iniquity that is carried from generation to generation.

Proverbs 22:8a says, *"He who sows iniquity* [evel (Hebrew)—perverseness, unrighteousness, iniquity, and wickedness], *will reap sorrow* [aven (Hebrew)—trouble, affliction, wickedness, iniquity, sorrow, mourning, and emptiness]..." In Hebrew, the link between evil and its effects and penalty are inseparable. *"...I, the Lord your God, am a jealous God, visiting the iniquity of the fathers upon the children to the third and fourth generations of those who hate Me"* **(Ex. 20:5b)**.

Areas of Iniquity

There are many areas of iniquity mentioned in Scripture that still affect us today. We should allow the Holy Spirit to convict us as we read the Bible, leading us to repent and confess these areas of sin. There are a few pages of patterns of iniquity in Appendix D. Take time to pray through them, and when appropriate, use them as ministry tools in praying with others.

As an example, you can see many areas of iniquity underlined in Isaiah 59.

"Behold, the Lord's hand is not shortened that it cannot save; nor His ear heavy, that it cannot hear. But your ***iniquities*** *have separated you from your God; and your sins have hidden His face from you, so that He will not hear. For your hands are defiled with blood, and your fingers with* ***iniquity****; your lips have spoken lies, your tongue has muttered perversity. No one calls for justice, nor does any plead for truth. They trust in empty words and speak lies; they conceive evil and bring forth* ***iniquity****... Their works are works of* ***iniquity****, and the act of violence is in their hands. Their feet run to evil, and they make haste to shed innocent blood; their thoughts are thoughts of* ***iniquity****; wasting and destruction are in their paths. The way of peace they have not known, and there is no justice in their ways; they have made themselves crooked paths; whoever takes that way shall not know peace... For our transgressions are multiplied before You, and our sins testify against us; for our transgressions are with us, and as for our* ***iniquities****, we know them: in transgressing and lying against the Lord, and departing from our God, speaking oppression and revolt, conceiving and uttering from the heart words of falsehood"* **(Isa. 59:1-4, 6b-8, 12-13)**.

Iniquity and its punishment are too heavy to be born by fallen man, so God sent Jesus to bear our iniquities for us. Like Cain who said in **Genesis 4:13**, *"My punishment* [avon—iniquity] *is greater than I can bear,"* the iniquity we are born with is also greater than we can bear!

"If You, Lord, should mark iniquities, O Lord, who could stand? But there is forgiveness with You, that You may be feared" (**Ps. 130:3-4**). It is scriptural to pray for freedom from iniquity. David did so in Psalm 51:2, 9; 119:133; and 40:11-13. Asaph prayed for mercy and deliverance from iniquities in Psalm 79:8-9. Moses prayed for pardon for iniquity in Numbers 14:18-19.

Isaiah 53:5-6 reveals that the Messiah was bruised for our iniquities and our rebellion. The Hebrew word translated "bruised" literally means to beat to pieces, to crush or destroy, and to humble. Jesus, our Messiah, was severely beaten to remove iniquity from us; He was crushed to cleanse it from our DNA and our lives. He doesn't merely forgive our sin; He also removes the iniquitous bent that we are born with! He gives us a new nature; we are new creations in Him—a whole new species (*see* **2 Cor. 5:17**).

Isaiah 53:11 tells us that Jesus bore our iniquities—our sin and our punishment for sin. Praying into the issue of iniquity is like all other areas of the atonement: although Jesus provided for our full salvation by His death and resurrection, we must appropriate what He did through believing, confessing, and applying these truths. *"...if you confess with your mouth the Lord Jesus and believe in your heart that God has raised Him from the dead, you will be saved. For with the heart one believes to righteousness, and with the mouth confession is made unto salvation"* (**Rom. 10:9-10**).

Breaking Curses Connected with Iniquity

Cancelling curses over yourself or others has limited effect if the iniquity has not been removed. Iniquity is the record of all the sins committed by prior generations. This information is not normally removed through a general prayer, like: *"Lord, please remove all of my iniquities."* Rather, it is important to identify the root of iniquity that initially and subsequently produced the curses. Then uproot each area of iniquity from your life through confession and prayer. Declare your freedom from it. Once you have done this, you can revoke and cancel the curses.

Steps to Freedom

If you are aware that you have particular inclinations toward certain sins, make a list of those sin patterns. Then list those of your parents and ancestors (which may be similar or the same). Remember to use Appendix D to make a thorough list. Confess the iniquities of your ancestors and your own transgressions, repenting of each sin by name. Ask the Lord for forgiveness and cleansing. Ask Him to wash all iniquity from your natural and spiritual DNA, and to heal all scarring there. This will take time, but it is worth it!

"We have sinned with our fathers, we have committed iniquity, we have done wickedly" (**Ps. 106:6**). *"Blessed is he whose transgression is forgiven, whose sin is covered. Blessed is the man to whom the Lord does not impute iniquity, and in whose spirit there is no deceit. When I kept silent, my bones grew old through my groaning all the day long. For day and night Your hand was heavy upon me; my vitality was turned into the drought of summer. I acknowledged my sin to You, and my iniquity I have not hidden. I said, 'I will confess my transgressions to the Lord,' and You forgave the iniquity of my sin"* (**Ps. 32:1-5**).

"O Israel, return to the Lord your God, for you have stumbled because of your iniquity; take words with you, and return to the Lord. Say to Him, "Take away all iniquity; receive us graciously, for we will offer the sacrifices of our lips..." " (**Hos. 14:1-2**).

Suggested Prayer

"Lord Jesus, thank You for bearing my iniquities—my tendencies toward evil, sin, moral illness, perversion, and crookedness. I confess to You my sins and iniquities. (Name them: pride, unbelief, deceit, theft, sins of the tongue, immorality...) *I confess the iniquity of my fathers and forefathers* (the same or other than the ones you confessed personally). *Please forgive the iniquity of our sin! Cleanse my spiritual DNA from all family iniquity and the sins of my forefathers, and heal all scarring on the strands of my DNA.*

"Break the power of iniquity off of my life and purge it from my spirit, soul, and body. I receive freedom and healing from all iniquity in the name of Jesus! I claim freedom from my generations!

"Thank You, Jesus, for bearing my iniquities and for allowing Yourself to be crushed so that I could have peace. Today, I appropriate what You did on the cross. Thank You for forgiving me and setting me free. Thank you for cleansing my bloodline and conscience with your blood and setting me apart for Yourself. I forgive everyone who has offended me, sinned against me, or wounded me in any way. I forgive those who sinned against my forefathers. Please cleanse all unforgiveness and bitterness from my DNA and my soul. I release forgiveness to all, and I receive the physical healing that is mine as I forgive. In Jesus' name, amen."

Stand Fast in Freedom!

"Blessed are the undefiled in the way, who walk in the law of the Lord! Blessed are those who keep His testimonies, who seek Him with the whole heart! They also do no iniquity; they walk in His ways" (**Ps. 119:1-3**).

To stay free from iniquity…

- Walk blamelessly before the Lord.
- Live according to His law and keep His commandments.
- Refuse to engage in rebellion of any kind. Resist temptation in the areas where you have been vulnerable to it in the past.
- Stay humble before God; resist pride and unbelief.
- Seek the Lord with *all* of your heart.

"Bless the Lord, O my soul; and all that is within me, bless His holy name... Who forgives all your iniquities, who heals all your diseases" (**Ps. 103:1, 3**).

EIGHTEEN

The Power of Forgiveness

"The Lord is merciful and gracious, slow to anger, and abounding in mercy. He will not always strive with us, nor will He keep His anger forever. He has not dealt with us according to our sins, nor punished us according to our iniquities. For as the heavens are high above the earth, so great is His mercy toward those who fear Him; as far as the east is from the west, so far has He removed our transgressions from us" **(Ps. 103:8-12)**. *"...if you forgive men their trespasses, your heavenly Father will also forgive you. But if you do not forgive men their trespasses, neither will your Father forgive your trespasses"* **(Matt. 6:14-15)**.

A little boy in Sunday school was heard to pray, *"...and forgive us our trash baskets as we forgive those who trash basket against us."*

Forgiveness is always two-fold: receiving forgiveness from God and forgiving others for their sins against us. Forgiveness is the bedrock of our faith and foundational in God's kingdom, so we must learn to give and receive it. Humility is the attitude by which we do both.

A relationship of any depth is a crash course in discovering one's own inadequacies. Most people who seek counsel are looking for help as they try to relate to God, resolve interpersonal conflicts, and attempt to build godly relationships. In order to offer wise counsel, it is vital that you know what the Bible says about relationships. I suggest you study the books of Proverbs, Ephesians, and Colossians. Because receiving and giving forgiveness is one of the chief components of meaningful relationships, we will look at these issues at length in this chapter.

Receiving Forgiveness

Jesus paid the full penalty for sin, enabling us to receive the gift of forgiveness from God when we humbly ask for it, confess our sin, and repent. *"For You, Lord, are good, and ready to forgive, and abundant in mercy to all who call upon You"* **(Ps. 86:5)**.

God described Himself in **Exodus 34:6-7** saying, *"...the Lord passed before him* [Moses] *and proclaimed, 'The Lord, the Lord God, merciful and gracious, longsuffering, and abounding in goodness and truth, keeping mercy for thousands, forgiving iniquity and sin and transgression, by no means clearing the guilty, visiting the iniquity of the fathers upon the children and the children's children to the third and the fourth generation."*

Even though there may be natural consequences for sin, the blood of Jesus is sufficient for ALL sin—past, present, and future. If the enemy reminds us of confessed sin, we can resist him because our sin has been placed under the blood of Jesus. When we refuse to receive God's forgiveness, we spurn His grace. When we do that: (1) our loved ones are at risk. Wallowing in guilt, we tend to be more withdrawn and critical, and less affectionate and open. So our families, co-workers, friends, and even our pets suffer along with us. (2) Our health is at risk. Doctors say bitterness generates chemicals that affect our vital organs. They increase our heart rate, raise our blood pressure, disrupt our digestion, tense our muscles, dump cholesterol into our bloodstream, and reduce our ability to think clearly. Science is now confirming that those who don't forgive themselves or others are more prone to heart attacks, depression, hypertension, and other serious illnesses.

Releasing Others

Once we have known God's mercy and received His forgiveness, we can more easily forgive others. We forgive the same way we are forgiven—with humility and faith. When we are hurt, offended, or treated badly, we meekly forgive, knowing we deserve far worse. Once forgiveness is extended, emotional pain can be healed and deliverance from demonic strongholds and oppression is possible. *Forgiveness is the key to inner healing.*

The Damage of Unforgiveness

Until we forgive, we are bound to the past and unable to live fully in the present. Our bitterness can both contaminate and damage our relationships.

When we retain hurt, we bind ourselves to the ones who inflicted the pain; we develop negative soul ties to them. By focusing on the wrong done and clinging to the pain or anger, we are chained to the people and the incidents, and we limit God's working in us and in them. It is as if we tie God's hands. But as soon as we forgive, God is released to work in their lives as well as in ours.

According to Matthew 18:34-35, unforgiveness provides an open door to the enemy. The tormentors who are assigned to those who refuse to release debts include depression, fear, doubt, strife, and disease. When we withhold mercy, we become susceptible to demonic harassment and oppression; unforgiveness eats away at our emotional, mental, and physical health. It is like drinking poison and expecting the person who wronged us to die.

When we refuse to forgive, we set into motion a downward cycle of progressive sin: unforgiveness grows into resentment; resentment matures into bitterness, which leads to blame and develops into hatred. Hatred results in rebellion, which causes a susceptibility to deception and self-deception. When a person is deceived, he is prone to perversion and other moral sins. In this day of increased deception, we should close every door that makes us vulnerable to it!

Bitter Root Judgments

Unforgiveness will hinder our spiritual growth faster than anything else. It can sometimes be hidden, but once it has developed a root of bitterness, it comes out in our speech, actions, reactions, and attitudes, and defiles others. **Hebrews 12:15** says, *"looking carefully lest anyone fall short of the grace of God; lest any root of bitterness springing up cause trouble, and by this many become defiled."*

A person with a root of bitterness is easily hurt and offended. He overreacts to minor injustices and takes on the offenses of others. Judgmental, he speaks harshly and critically. Bitterness is the seedbed for any demonic work! The works of the flesh found in Galatians 5:19-21 can be traced back to bitterness and back further to hurt or rejection.

Authors and teachers, John and Paula Sandford, coined the phrase *"bitter root judgments,"* which means: what we judge in others will manifest in us. When we bitterly focus on a person's sin and judge him for it, we run the risk of developing that same sin in ourselves. This principle is stated positively in 2 Corinthians 3:18. As we behold the glory of the Lord, we are changed into His image from glory to glory. The more we gaze at Him, the more we are transformed into His likeness.

What we are often quick to see in others is either already within us or there is potential for it to be there. *"... you are inexcusable...whoever you are who judge, for in whatever you judge another you condemn yourself; for you who judge practice the same thing*s" (**Rom. 2:1**).

A common cause of marital dysfunction is when a spouse carries bitterness from a former romantic relationship into the marriage. He will tend to react within the new relationship out of his old wounds. This can be seen in most second marriages. Unless significant forgiveness and healing take place from the first failed relationship, one entering a second one has unresolved issues and bitterness to overcome as well as the normal adjustments to make which a relationship of commitment requires.

Anticipating rejection within a new relationship can cause such anxiety that a person breaks off the relationship before the other one can. Self-protecting and self-centered, he insensitively removes others from his life too easily. He struggles to see beyond the walls of his own little world.

Forgiveness: Choice not Feeling

We must choose to extend forgiveness by faith, willfully releasing the past. The *feelings* of forgiveness come later. Emotions that have been trained and disciplined will follow the will (rather than dictate to it) and might lag behind temporarily. Emotions need nourishment from God's Word (*see* **Ps. 107:20**) and time to heal. We need to soak in the Scriptures and receive God's healing love to be restored and to retain our healing. When we can pray for and bless our offenders, we know that our emotions have caught up with our choice of forgiveness.

The flesh loves to hold onto hurt and anger. Part of dying to self is releasing all transgressions committed against us by anyone. A corpse feels no pain and seeks no revenge. If we are really dead to self and alive to God, we can handle others' debts to us as He handles ours—by forgiving them. *"And you, being dead in your trespasses and the uncircumcision of your flesh, He has made alive together with Him, having forgiven you all trespasses, having wiped out the handwriting of requirements that was against us, which was contrary to us. And He has taken it out of the way, having nailed it to the cross*" (**Col. 2:13-14**). We must forgive even if we never receive an apology, explanation, or restitution. We "put it behind us" like God Who puts our sins behind His back (*see* **Isa. 38:17**). We choose never to look at the offense again. If the devil reminds us of it, we resist him, and bless those who hurt us. Forgiving enables us to look forward rather than backward.

Building Relationships of Trust

Forgiveness is spiritual warfare. It undermines Satan's plan to accuse, blame, or torment. It heals and builds the Body of Messiah. Refusing to forgive will hinder spiritual growth faster than anything else. Do not allow yourself the luxury of retaining hurt and bitterness; it isn't worth it. Sometimes confrontation is needed in order to restore the relationship. When we repress and overlook offenses without confronting those who offended us, we tend to withdraw and close our hearts from them. To be one in Messiah, we need relationships of trust. We should love others enough to seek understanding and restoration. Once we forgive, we should never mention the hurt again.

Cope with or overcome?

Some psychologists encourage people not to forgive in order not to show weakness. They teach them how to cope with hurt and anger. Jesus commands us to forgive, and by that, to *overcome* offense. "Cope" is not part of His vocabulary; "overcome" is. To overcome, we have to die to ourselves and to all hope of revenge.

We are to "die daily," and to be able to say with the Apostle Paul, *"It is no longer I who live, but Christ lives in me; and the life which I now live in the flesh I live by the faith of the Son of God, who loved me and gave Himself for me"* (**Gal. 2:20b**, KJV).

A Pattern for Forgiving

Make a list of all people (living or deceased) who offended or hurt you. Then forgive each one by name. (*"I forgive _________ for his offense of ______."*) Release your resentment toward the Lord if you are angry with Him.

Confess to God your carnal, selfish ways of handling hurt and your refusal to forgive and reconcile with others. *"If we confess our sins, He is faithful and just to forgive us our sins and to cleanse us from all unrighteousness"* (**1 John 1:9**).

Martin Luther, the great Reformer, in one of his periods of depression, seemed to see a hideous form inscribing the record of his own transgressions on the walls of his room. The accusing hand wrote down the sinful words and thoughts, evil deeds, sins of omission and commission, secret sins, and open sins. There seemed to be no end of them. Luther bowed his head in prayer. When he looked up again, the writer had paused and was facing him. *"Thou hast forgotten just one thing!"* said Luther. *"And that?"* queried his tormentor. *"Take thy pen once more and write across it all: 'The blood of Jesus Christ his Son cleanseth us from all sin!'"* And, at the mention of the blood of Jesus, the evil spirit vanished and the walls were clean.

To help you appropriate God's forgiveness, it might help you to look in the mirror and say to yourself, *"I forgive you for ___________."* Cremate your past; don't embalm it! Once you have forgiven, you can command all tormentors to leave: fear, depression, anxiety, illness, etc. Ask the Lord what you should resist in Jesus' name, and then with the authority He has given you, do so!

Repenting of Bitterness

Even after we forgive, the root of bitterness may be lodged within our souls. It is removed through repentance and renunciation. If we do not deal with the bitterness, the fruit of offense may grow again quickly. Bitterness gives ground to the enemy in our lives; he has a legal stronghold until we repent and give that ground back to Jesus. So, acknowledge bitterness as sin. Confess it to God and renounce it in Jesus' name. Then claim Jesus' blood for it, thanking Him that His blood is sufficient for *all* sin. Ask the Lord to retake the ground of your heart, to destroy the stronghold of bitterness, and to establish His rule again within you.

Ask God what other areas of sin you need to confess to Him. List those sins and ask Jesus to forgive you. (*"I confess my sin of __________ to You, and ask You to forgive me" or "I am sorry I did __________ to ____________. Please forgive me."*)

Once you have made things right with the Lord, be reconciled with the people you wronged. Make restitution where necessary; if you broke or damaged something, pay for it or replace it. Holiness and righteous living must follow forgiveness, for God is not content merely to erase our past; He wants to establish our future in Him.

Jesus expressed perfect forgiveness by not accusing those who betrayed or crucified Him after His resurrection. When we walk in that level of forgiveness, we will do the same: we will forgive even while being persecuted or harassed, and we will never mention the offense again. When we surrender our hurt and pain to Jesus, we do just that—we *surrender* it!

"Who is a God like You, pardoning iniquity and passing over the transgression of the remnant of His heritage? He does not retain His anger forever, because He delights in mercy. He will again have compassion on us, and will subdue our iniquities. You will cast all our sins into the depths of the sea" (**Mic. 7:18-19**).

NINETEEN

Reconciled and Restored Relationships

"...if you bring your gift to the altar, and there remember that your brother has something against you, leave your gift there before the altar, and go your way. First be reconciled to your brother, and then come and offer your gift" (**Matt. 5:23-24**). *"If possible, so far as it depends on you, be at peace with all men"* (**Rom. 12:18**, NASB).

Right or righteous?

God sets a very high priority on harmonious relationships. In His order, worshiping Him is to come *after* restoration with people. If you know that someone has something against you, go to that person as soon as possible and be reconciled. Whether or not you are guilty is not important if the wounded person has *perceived* you as guilty. Who is right or wrong does not matter so long as reconciliation occurs. If you insist on standing in your *rightness*, you might sacrifice walking in Jesus' *righteousness*.

If someone has hurt or offended *you*, it is also up to you to initiate restoration. You might say to the person: *"Are you at peace with me? Have I offended you in some way? Be honest with me; I value your friendship."* Eliminate the word "if" in the reconciliation process ("*If* I hurt you..."). This small word will make restoration more difficult because the wounded person will feel you are insensitive to his hurt. Saying "if" demonstrates a sense of innocence regarding the offense.

Instructions for Seeking Reconciliation

"Moreover if your brother sins against you, go and tell him his fault between you and him alone. If he hears you, you have gained your brother. But if he will not hear, take with you one or two more, that 'by the mouth of two or three witnesses every word may be established.' And if he refuses to hear them, tell it to the church. But if he refuses even to hear the church, let him be to you like a heathen and a tax collector" (**Matt. 18:15-17**).

1. Speak to the person alone. *"Debate your case with your neighbor, and do not disclose the secret to another"* (**Prov. 25:9**). The person at fault has the right to hear first (unless you need pastoral guidance). Do not tell others to get them on your side. When you tell others before you tell the one who hurt you, you create problems:

• You prove to God and others that you do not love the offender. You also demonstrate that you do not love the Lord, because you have disobeyed His command to go to the offender alone.

• You tempt your listener to take up an offense against the offender, damaging a possible friendship between them. This is spreading discord and disunity among brothers—a sin God hates, according to Proverbs 6. *"...a whisperer separates the best of friends"* (**Prov. 16:28**).

• When you eventually approach the one who hurt you, he may question your sincerity, which reduces the potential for restoration.

Avoid quoting others to strengthen your point by saying things like: *"Others have said the same thing about you"* or *"The pastor sees this in you, too."* Quoting other people brings condemnation to the person and breeds discord in the Body of Messiah.

In Luke 17:3-4, Jesus said to speak to the one who sinned against you before you forgive him. Mature love will confront and forgive because it desires wholeness in the other person as well as a restored relationship. When we forgive without reconciling, we close our hearts from trusting further, and the relationship is seldom as open and healthy as before.

2. Take one or two <u>mutual</u> friends with you who can listen objectively and confirm what was said or done.

Throughout the confrontation, make sure you show the Lord's heart of mercy. Be willing to forgive whether or not the person repents. Our standard of forgiving is found in **Ephesians 4:32**, *"...forgiving one another even as God in Christ forgave you."*

3. Tell the congregational leadership and enlist their help in achieving restoration if the person still refuses to be reconciled.

Throughout the process, involve as few people as possible and examine yourself before you approach the person. Jesus tells us in Matthew 7:5 to get the plank out of our own eyes before we try to get a speck out of someone else's.

If we obey Jesus' words in Matthew 18, we can expect gossip and slander in the Body of Messiah to cease. As we speak graciously to one another, the Church will be edified and strengthened. Expressed loyalties will build security and a defense against suspicion, and the world will believe that Jesus is God's Messiah (*see* **John 17:21**).

Care for your relationships

Take good care of your relationships! Deal with conflict quickly; do not procrastinate in seeking reconciliation. Merely hoping everything will be fine usually results in things *not* being all right for too long. Make every effort to be reconciled with everyone! If it is a brother with whom you are at odds, be restored to him before trying to minister to the Lord. If you have a broken relationship with an unbeliever, deal with the situation as soon as possible to avoid future problems and repercussions. *"Agree with your adversary quickly, while you are on the way with him, lest your adversary deliver you to the judge, the judge hand you over to the officer, and you be thrown in prison"* (**Matt. 5:25**).

"Pursue peace with all people, and holiness, without which no one will see the Lord" (**Heb. 12:14a**). If we are not holy and unified with one another in the Body of Messiah, no one will see Jesus (in us). What a responsibility we have! Let's watch over one another with godly zeal and be serious about our ministry of reconciliation.

"Now all things are of God, who has reconciled us to Himself through Jesus Christ, and has given us the ministry of reconciliation" (**2 Cor. 5:18**).

TWENTY

Recognizing Demonic Oppression

"And when He had called His twelve disciples to Him, He gave them power over unclean spirits, to cast them out, and to heal all kinds of sickness and all kinds of disease... "As you go, preach, saying, 'The kingdom of heaven is at hand.' Heal the sick, cleanse the lepers, raise the dead, cast out demons. Freely you have received, freely give" (**Matt. 10:1, 7-8**). *"Behold, I give you the authority to trample on serpents and scorpions, and over all the power of the enemy, and nothing shall by any means hurt you. Nevertheless, do not rejoice in this, that the spirits are subject to you, but rather rejoice because your names are written in heaven"* (**Luke 10:19-20**).

Jesus specifically commanded His disciples to cast out demons as part of their ministry. That command is still in effect today. Deliverance can be an unpleasant, challenging, and taxing ministry, but as Jesus' disciples, we must be willing to go into dark places to release prisoners of demonic affliction from their captivity.

Descriptions of Demons

1. Demons are disembodied spirits and seek bodies to inhabit. Many demons can oppress one person (*see* **Luke 8:27, 30**). Restless outside a body, they often inhabit animals if they cannot inhabit humans.

2. Demons behave like their master, Satan. They steal peace, joy, and health; they kill and destroy (*see* **John 10:10**).

3. Demons are proud and want to be recognized. They are filthy, vile, and physically strong (*see* **Mark 5:3-5**).

4. Demons are attracted to unclean objects (*see* **Deut. 7:26**) and to literature about false religions and the occult. Such objects should be burned when prayerfully cleansing a house from demonic oppression.

5. Demons are subject to God's people who are walking in victory. (*see* **Luke 10:19**)

It is possible for believers to be afflicted or oppressed by evil spirits. If a believer is trying to walk uprightly, but has incomplete victory with troubled and defeated areas in his life, and/or if he feels compelled to destructive acts, he may need a measure of deliverance.

In ministering deliverance, it is helpful to determine the sins, wounds, and offenses that have made the person vulnerable to demonic influences. Rather than merely confronting surface sins and the fruit of iniquity in one's life, we should look for root causes and possible demonic infestation. When possible, it is beneficial to research one's family history, childhood experiences, and relationships to get a full picture of the ministry needed (see Appendices A and E for guidelines and questions).

Information to Gather

Physical: Ask the counselee about any possible addictions, eating habits (to make sure the issue does not result from a poor diet), medication (which can account for depression or hallucinations), and sleeping problems (nightmares or insomnia). Ask if he/she was abused in any way (physical, emotional, verbal, or sexual). Does he have any unusual physical habits or hang-ups that you should know about (such as cross-dressing)?

Mental: Does he have obsessive, uncontrollable thoughts? Murderers have testified to hearing voices say, *"Kill him! Kill him!"* Does he have tormenting fears? Does he have unclean thoughts about God during worship services or personal devotions? Is he oppressed while he prays? Does he have a mental block when he reads the Bible? Does he have obsessive suicidal thoughts? Most people consider suicide at one time or another, but demonized individuals often have persistent and tormenting thoughts of suicide.

What kind of reading material, music, movies, and TV programs does he watch or listen to? The media is a common open door for the enemy to tempt and attack in areas of fear, lust, violence, perversion, and rebellion. Does he hear voices? Demons commonly speak to one's mind: accusing, tempting, and planting their ideas.

Mentally ill people are normally quick to talk about voices and spirits; a demonized person typically will speak less about spirits as they prefer to stay hidden. In some cases, demons attach to and aggravate a true mental condition of schizophrenia or other psychoses. Mental disorders tend to have predictable patterns with observable symptoms. A person with a mental illness usually responds positively to prayer, medication, psychiatric treatment, and counseling. A demonized person will not show long-term improvement from any of these means.

Emotional: Does he have debilitating fears that prevent him from living a normal life? Does he have compulsions or obsessions (e.g., washing one's hands 25 times a day or checking the handbrake a dozen times while driving)? Does he have unhealthy soul-ties, codependent relationships, or share inordinate affection with friends?

Spiritual: Is he sure of his salvation? Occasional doubts are normal, but irrational doubts and accusations against God's character can reveal a spirit of unbelief. Has he treated his struggles as sin through repentance, confession, applying the Word, discipline, and prayer, and yet still feel in bondage in those areas?

Does he have any interest in or involvement with the occult or cults? Does he use alternative New Age medicines that are based in Eastern religions or connected with witchcraft? Does he use martial arts? Martial arts are founded in ancient oriental religions, and the actions used and words shouted are part of the worship of the spirits behind those religions. Even when participants are ignorant of these things, the demons take advantage of them since they are in their territory. Some of the words shouted are names of foreign gods (demons) and are invitations to demonic oppression. Many believers who begin innocently in martial arts later feel convicted to abandon these sports. We are to judge something by its fruit; the fruit of martial arts is normally violence, self-protection, and pride.

Family History: Were his parents or grandparents involved in the occult? Psychic abilities are often passed down through the bloodline. Was he involved in a counterfeit religion or a cult? Deceiving spirits and idolatry are passed down. Is there a history of mental illness in the family? Were there problems of addiction? The addictions may vary, but the spirit of bondage is the same. Was there harmony in the home? If not, this can reveal spirits of strife, jealousy, and violence. Are adultery or divorces common in the extended family? Spirits of lust, adultery, and division run in families.

Was he or she adopted? There are often family curses, iniquity, and unclean spirits passed down from biological parents and grandparents. A spirit of rejection often oppresses a person who was adopted.

What was the moral climate in the home? Was there incest? Sexual perversions? What movies and reading material were available? Were healthy boundaries taught and modeled? Spirits of lust and perversion are often passed down through family iniquity. Home environments are not as safe and moral as they used to be. Here are only a few of the situations I have encountered through counseling:

• A young teenager had an addiction to pornography because she was taking her father's magazines from his bathroom and enjoying them in her room alone.

• A lady had distorted ideas of sexual intimacy because her father made his family watch pornographic videos together at home as the children were growing up.

• A young lady slept in her mother's bedroom when she was a child, watching her mother "entertain" paying guests as a prostitute.

These stories would be sad enough if they were isolated incidents, but similar situations are multiplied over and over in these days of rampant evil.

If the counselee has a problem with gluttony, anorexia or other food disorders, try to find out if the behavior was modeled or encouraged in the home before you assume that demons are involved. Anorexia can reveal a lack of parental affirmation or a deep wound by an authority figure (father, teacher, or coach). It can be a reaction to "fat" comments made by authorities. Such comments may seem innocent, but they can cause self-rejection and even lead to a spirit of death.

Other Key Questions and Behaviors to Observe

1. Has he been oppressed by evil or destructive emotions that are contrary to his own will or nature (e.g., hatred, anger, fear, pride, or jealousy)? Severe personality changes may indicate demonic strongholds (e.g., a kind lady who flies into a rage and beats her children. Later she regretfully says, *"I don't know what came over me."*).

2. Is he restless, excessively talkative, or unreasonable? Do his moods fluctuate dramatically, especially when you address spiritual matters, pray, read Scripture, or mention the name or blood of Jesus? Discern between hyperactivity (ADD, ADHD) and demonic frenzy.

3. Is he experiencing deep depression and irrational, suicidal self-pity?

4. Is he enslaved to sexual immorality or deviancy? Does he have uncontrollable unclean thoughts? Is he enslaved to alcohol, nicotine, or drugs? Slavery reveals demonic oppression. Key words are *enslaved* and *uncontrollable.*

5. Does he uncontrollably use profanity or unclean language, mock others during worship, or blaspheme God?

6. Is he preoccupied with sexually perverse, violent, or demonic practices?

Points of Demonic Entry

Demons gain a foothold in a person's life through a number of means. The point of entry may require specific repentance and/or healing prayers that will coincide with prayers for deliverance. If the demon does not leave easily, ask the Lord how it gained entrance into the person's life. Praying into the point of entry can be the key to casting out resistant spirits.

I prayed for a woman oppressed by a spirit of death. Her hands were around her throat and she was struggling to breathe. I quoted relevant Scriptures and rebuked the spirit in Jesus' name, and yet it resisted.

Beginning to feel desperate, I asked the Lord for a word of knowledge. He showed me that she had Freemasonry in her background, and that an ancestor of hers had been hung. I prayed into the entry points, confessing the Freemasonry of her ancestors as sin and breaking the power of it off of her life. Then I confessed the sin of the hanging murder, and we forgave those who were guilty. Following that, the spirit could be easily cast out. The points of entry had been closed.

Common Points of Entry

1. natural appetites indulged to excess — Overeating or engaging in illicit sexual activity can provide an open door to spirits of bondage, gluttony, or immorality. *"Do you not know that to whom you present yourselves slaves to obey, you are that one's slaves whom you obey, whether of sin leading to death, or of obedience leading to righteousness?"* (**Rom. 6:16**)

2. habitual sin — Habitual sin can lead to an addiction and demonic oppression. (Children that are allowed to throw temper tantrums may give entry to spirits of anger and/or violence.) Addictions may not always indicate demonic activity, but spirits of bondage commonly enter where there is an addiction.

3. trauma, serious illness, hurt, or fear — When our natural protection is down and we are weak emotionally or physically, the enemy can attempt invasion (i.e., a car accident, a divorce, a bad fall, witnessing a violent death, or a major illness).

Denise had suffered from severe depression for 16 years. It robbed her of health, and negatively affected her outlook on life and her walk with God. She had no joy. She disliked worship services as she could not praise the Lord freely as others did. Researching her history, I discovered that she had spent a year in the hospital as a child. Frightened and alone there, she was vulnerable to oppression from a spirit of heaviness (**Isa. 61:3**). The trauma and illness she experienced lowered her guard, and she was helpless against an evil spirit that afflicted her for years following. When Jesus delivered her, she shouted with victory, laughed, and praised Him. A few years later, she was still joyful, praising God easily, and had no symptoms of depression.

4. sexual sin — Spirits of lust, adultery, and perversion can be transferred through illicit sexual relationships. Sexual exploration with others, sexual abuse, pornography, sexual fantasies, ungodly soul ties, and fornication can result in demonic oppression.

5. occultic family background — This gives easy access to the enemy through one's bloodline as well as through the home environment.

6. personal involvement in the occult — This is a direct invitation to evil spirits. Playing occult computer games, reading occult material (e.g., horoscope books), going to a fortune-teller, receiving prayer from a psychic healer, being hypnotized, or possessing occult objects are invitations to demons. All occult practices are abominable to God (*see* **Lev. 20:6, Gal. 5:19-21**).

7. false religions and cults — These open doors to spirits of deception, religion, and unbelief.

8. prenatal influences — A fetus is vulnerable chiefly through the mother, although he can receive spiritual inheritance from both parents. Spirits of rejection, fear, adultery, lust, and witchcraft are the common spirits that gain access to a fetus. When a pregnancy is unwanted, a spirit of rejection may oppress the child from birth.

During a general prayer time for inner healing at a youth camp, a young lady wailed loudly while being delivered from a spirit of rejection. She later testified that she was unwanted from her conception and had felt rejected all of her life. As the spirit was cast out and her emotions began to be healed, she felt accepted and loved by God for the first time.

9. parental domination and manipulation — These can indirectly lead to demonic oppression by stunting the normal emotional development of the child. He may become aggressive and rebellious, or he may hate himself and others and fear failure.

10. failure to forgive — Holding onto resentment can lead to rebellion, deception, and moral perversion.

11. yielding control of one's mind — A passive mind renders us vulnerable to the enemy (e.g., hypnotism or transcendental meditation). The Scriptures command us to be alert and to keep our minds ready for action (*see* **1 Pet. 1:13**). Meditation in God's Word is powerfully beneficial (*see* **Ps. 1:2**), but other meditations must be avoided.

12. generational influences — The sin of one generation "uncovers" the next generation. As said before, family curses or spirits are passed down through the spiritual bloodline of the forefathers (*see* **Ex. 20:5**).

13. death — Familiar spirits leave their human home when the person dies and look for another home—preferably a family member of the deceased. Having an abortion can open the door to a spirit of murder.

Cindy had had an abortion as a young lady. Years later, she confessed to hating pregnant women so intensely that she wanted to cut them open with a knife. She felt murderous rage toward children and wanted to hurt them. To be free, she needed deliverance from spirits of murder, hatred, and death. She also needed healing from the trauma of abortion and from the burden of guilt and shame.

When a baby is conceived following an abortion, the baby sometimes senses the death of the previous fetus and has unexplained feelings of grief or anger toward the mother. The baby might be born with a spirit of rejection, lust, rage, or death. If a previous baby was miscarried, the living child may feel unexplained grief and depression and may need deliverance from a spirit of heaviness.

14. curses — Curses, a common entry points for demons, can be self-imposed word curses, curses from authorities, or curses by witches.

15. blood transfusions — Spirits that are attached to one's DNA or bloodline can strongly influence anyone who receives the blood. *"...the life of the flesh is in the blood"* (**Lev. 17:11a**).

16. demonically-inspired media — Watching horror films can open a door to a spirit of fear; listening to heavy rock music that glorifies the devil or watching shows where black magic or witchcraft is featured gives the enemy an easy entry.

Note: In formal Satanism, there are documented unholy days when certain rituals and sacrifices (animal and human) are performed. These are times of heightened evil activity when the Body of Messiah should enter into strong praise and worship to resist the plans of the enemy. The main dates are: Feb. 2–March 20 (spring equinox); April 26–May 1, June 21 (summer solstice); Aug. 3–Sept. 22 (fall equinox); Oct. 29–Nov.1 (All Hallow's Eve); and Dec. 22–24 (winter solstice).

Scriptures Regarding Casting Out Evil Spirits

- In Matthew 17:20-21, we see that faith is necessary in deliverance ministry. Fasting added to prayer is powerfully effective against demons (*see* **Isa. 58:6**).

- In Acts 16:16-18, the Apostle Paul put up with demonic harassment for days before casting out the spirit; then he spoke directly to the demon in the name of Jesus. Philippians 2:10-11, Matthew 7:22, and Luke 10:17 speak of the power of Jesus' name over demons.

- In Acts 8:6-7, the demons cried out as they left.

- In Mark 1:25, 34, Jesus did not let the demons speak. We, too, can command their silence.

- In Matthew 8:31-32, Jesus sent the demons into the pigs as they requested. The demons may have hurt their victim as they left if they weren't permitted another "home."

- In Luke 9:39-42, the Lord rebuked the spirit. He did not converse with it or let it speak. He healed the child, closing the door to the spirit's entry. Then He gave him back to his father, reinstating the father's authority over him in place of the demon's power over him.

"Then He called His twelve disciples together and gave them power and authority over all demons, *and to cure diseases"* **(Luke 9:1)**. *"For this purpose the Son of God was manifested, that He might destroy the works of the devil"* **(1 John 3:8b)**.

TWENTY-ONE

Hands-on Deliverance Ministry

"...if I cast out demons with the finger of God, surely the kingdom of God has come upon you" (**Luke 11:20**). *"Go into all the world and preach the gospel to every creature. And these signs will follow those who believe: In My name they will cast out demons; they will speak with new tongues; they will take up serpents; and if they drink anything deadly, it will by no means hurt them; they will lay hands on the sick, and they will recover"* (**Mark 16:15, 17-18**).

As disciples of Jesus, we are to preach the gospel, heal the sick, and cast out demons. It helps to know how to minister deliverance before we actually engage in it. This ministry and the healing of the soul go together. To cast out demons, we must have enough trust in the Lord that we are not afraid of or distracted by evil spirits. It is vital that we be sensitive to the leading of the Holy Spirit. Our emotions must be disciplined and our thoughts focused. Even if the issues we are counselling touch on troubled areas in our own hearts, we are to keep our emotions in check (submitted to God's Spirit) while we minister.

Deliverance ministry works best with teamwork; Jesus sent out His disciples two-by-two (**Luke 10:1**). When you know that casting out demons will be a part of a prayer session with someone, try to have an intercessor and/or a co-worker with you. Choose someone you trust and know fairly well; having a spiritual rapport with your ministry partner(s) with complementary spiritual gifts and natural strengths is a valuable asset. Some deliverance sessions require much time, patience, and energy; switching leadership during such sessions can be helpful and wise.

Imperatives

1. Recognize the power of the name and blood of Jesus. Memorize verses about the name and blood of Jesus so that you can easily quote them when praying with someone. Demons flee in response to hearing Jesus' name, not because of voice volume!

Pam's parents were high priests in Satanism, so she grew up being forced to attend satanic rituals. Torture was a normal part of her life. One day as a six-year-old, she was made to sit in a dark pit alone. Jesus appeared to her and sat down next to her in his white garment. She said to Him, *"You shouldn't sit here; you'll get dirty."* Jesus introduced Himself to her, and told her that if she would ask Him to come into her heart, He would do so and be her friend. She said, *"Oh, I want that! Please come into my heart!"* Soon afterward, while frightened during a satanic ritual, she cried out, *"Jesus, Jesus!"* for her Friend to help her. To her dismay, the witches covered their ears and screamed, running in small circles. Only when she was older and more mature in her faith did she realize that demons fear Jesus' name.

2. Stay under spiritual authority. Evil spirits recognize when you are under authority. If you are in rebellion to your spiritual coverings (parents if you're underage, husband, pastor), your protection is lacking and you may suffer a backlash from the enemy. If you have young children, attempt to keep them in subjection to you; the devil sometimes initiates counterattacks through rebellious children. Independent counselors in this ministry can be susceptible to deception and/or extra attack from the enemy.

3. Know your God-given authority. In **Luke 10:19**, Jesus said, *"Behold, I give you the authority to trample on serpents and scorpions, and over all the power of the enemy, and nothing shall by any means hurt you."* Don't be threatened by resisting spirits. Address them in the name of Jesus until they leave.

A well-known evangelist said, *"Until I understood the work of demons and the defeat of Satan, I feared to preach or speak concerning them, but now that I understand their work, I no longer fear them; rather, they fear me."*

Stronger spirits (principalities and powers) should not be confronted unwisely (e.g., Islamic spirits). Only a group of seasoned intercessors that has engaged in preparatory fasting and prayer should confront them, and then only by the Lord's clear leading.

4. Wear spiritual armor and maintain righteous relationships. Before going to battle for someone else, you should be victorious on a personal level. Seal all cracks in your spiritual armor that could make you vulnerable to attack. In **Ephesians 6:10**, the Apostle Paul wrote, *"Finally, my brethren, be strong in the Lord,"* and then he wrote about putting on spiritual armor. The subjects that precede the '*finally*' are relationships in the home, marriage, and church. If the enemy has a foothold in any of these areas, there must be repentance and restoration before one takes on the enemy. You can quote **Proverbs 26:2** (*"... a curse without cause shall not alight"*) frequently, and yet not realize that you are vulnerable to the enemy because of hurting relationships.

Pastor Ed Silvoso, an international intercessory leader, said, *"I have found that in every place where the Scriptures speak about spiritual warfare, it is always in conjunction with teaching about relationships."*

Put on the armor of God daily, praying over each piece mentioned in Ephesians 6:10-18. For example, while putting on the belt of truth, you can pray, *"Lord, help me to walk in truth today, to speak the truth in love, to live in integrity, and to discern truth from lies. Deliver me from all hypocrisy and deception."*

5. Keep your heart pure, free of known or deliberate sin. In the areas where you have full victory, expelling demons is easier. Don't attempt to minister deliverance with sin in your life (*see* **Ps. 66:18**). Because we discern by God's Spirit through our hearts, our discernment is impure if our hearts are impure. Once our hearts are clean, our discernment can be trusted. For instance, prejudice against the one you are ministering to can cause you to "discern" problems that are not really there. A pure heart enables you to hear the voice of the Holy Spirit clearly.

Suggested Procedure

1. Begin with general prayers. Appropriate the protection of Jesus' blood over yourself and the counselee, and over your families, homes, and possessions. Then lead him in prayers of forgiveness, repentance, and renunciation. This gives you a legal right to command demons to leave.

Deliberate sin or unforgiveness give spirits a right to stay because areas of darkness are relegated to them. Renouncing sin (especially the occult and perversions) shuts the door to the spirits' easy re-entry and shows them the counselee means business.

When ministering deliverance to a child, it is good to first engage in spiritual warfare and nullify the power of the demons afflicting the child before praying for him. This paves the way for a rapid deliverance, and causes minimal fear for the child if it's handled correctly. Include the parents in the spiritual warfare and intercession session if you can. You can pray for young children for deliverance while they sleep or play.

2. Authoritatively cast out evil spirits by name or by manifestation. Demons cannot read our minds, so we must confront them audibly. Once you know the counselee's situation, you will have a good idea what spirits are present simply by their revealed nature. Address the demon by its nature and manifestation. The name reflects the essence of the character, so either the actual name (e.g., "lying spirit") or its manifestation ("spirit that deceives and lies") is sufficient. Evil thrives in darkness and deception, and hates the truth and the light. Naming the spirit exposes it, weakens its hold, and sets the stage for deliverance.

Ruling spirits often gain a foothold through the sins of bitterness, rebellion, control, rejection, unbelief, pride, and lust. When these strong spirits are cast out, other demons are weakened and come out more easily.

3. Rely on the Holy Spirit to discern their departure. If we command demons to go quietly and not hurt the person they are afflicting, many will leave without much manifestation. Sometimes spirits may manifest and yet not leave, so a good way to be certain of their departure is to feel the witness in your spirit as prompted by the Holy Spirit. A peaceful look or a shout of joy from the person, a deep inner knowing that the demon is gone, or a tangible release felt in the room are signs that can be trusted more than a cough, shriek, or sigh from the one being delivered.

As hard as she tried, Sue couldn't hear God speak to her. When a small group of women began praying for her, Sue felt increasing pressure in her chest, squeezing her heart and lungs tightly. She heard voices, but could not hear God's voice. The women began to discern and cast out evil spirits, beginning with spirits of witchcraft. Sue admitted to having been involved in the occult, as had her ancestors. Other demons were addressed and cast out: spirits of death, lying, infirmity, and fear. She had been cursed as a child, so the women broke the curses over her in the name of Jesus. She repented of looking at pornography, and the spirit of lust was cast out. She cooperated with the women, confessing, repenting, and renouncing sin. Eventually, she shouted, *"I'm free! I feel clean!"* The women felt the freedom and release in the room, and knew Sue's deliverance was complete.

While being delivered, a counselee should refrain from speaking or singing with those praying for him. He can confess sin, claim the power of the name and blood of Jesus, and insist that the demons leave him, but he should keep his mouth free for departing spirits to leave that way. Many demons leave through the mouth.

The longer demons have oppressed a person, the more they may resist or manifest. A person with a consistent walk with the Lord can usually be delivered quickly and quietly when spirits are addressed.

Some demons leave during times of praise and worship. A new believer was excited in her new love relationship with Jesus and spent three weeks singing to Him in worship around her home. One day, she suddenly heard a male voice say through her mouth, *"I've had enough of this! I'm getting out of here!"* She ran to the toilet to vomit and felt an immediate release. She called her pastor to ask what had happened. He told her that she had just been delivered of an evil spirit.

4. Ask the Holy Spirit to fill all empty places in the person. If counselees are not yet baptized with the Spirit, teach them about the Holy Spirit and pray for them. Pray for a refilling if they were previously baptized with the Spirit. Vacated places within a person must be filled with the Holy Spirit. The temptations and warfare that follow deliverance must be fought in the power of the Spirit.

Hindrances to Successful Deliverance

1. unforgiveness — Candidates for deliverance must forgive everyone who has sinned against them.

2. involvement in occult practices, false religions, or cults — These must be confessed as sin and renounced; they give the enemy license to stay.

3. having had an abortion or having been party to one — Abortion is murder and must be confessed, and God's forgiveness received.

4. retaining the sin(s) that gave demons entrance — The sin(s) that gave the demons entrance must be confessed and repented of or those demon(s) can return with more powerful ones (*see* **Matt. 12:43-45**). If a demonized person does not want to be free of a particular controlling sin, then full deliverance is impossible. By choosing the sin, the person gives the demon permission to stay. All that the ministry team can do is intercede until the person repents.

5. unconfessed sexual sin — Adultery, fornication, homosexuality, and other areas of immorality must be confessed and renounced so that the enemy has no legal right to stay.

Deny the Flesh and Resist the Devil

You cannot cast out the flesh or crucify the devil. You crucify and deny the flesh, and you resist the devil. If demons are oppressing or binding you in some way, get rid of them! Don't just try to subdue them!

If you believe you need a measure of deliverance, pray for yourself or find someone to pray with you. Once you have been freed from demonic influences, subduing the flesh in those areas will be much easier. Many believers testify to this.

Demons harass believers to minimize their effectiveness and spiritual growth. The aim of deliverance is to remove these trespassing spirits from one's soul and body so that Jesus can reign totally in the believer's life. I am firmly convinced that deliverance ministry is needed in the Body of Messiah today.

"Then I heard a loud voice saying in heaven, 'Now salvation, and strength, and the kingdom of our God, and the power of His Christ have come, for the accuser of our brethren, who accused them before our God day and night, has been cast down. And they overcame him by the blood of the Lamb and by the word of their testimony, and they did not love their lives to the death'" (**Rev. 12:10-11**).

TWENTY-TWO

Retaining Freedom from Demonic Oppression

"When an unclean spirit goes out of a man, he goes through dry places, seeking rest, and finds none. Then he says, 'I will return to my house from which I came.' And when he comes, he finds it empty, swept, and put in order. Then he goes and takes with him seven other spirits more wicked than himself, and they enter and dwell there; and the last state of that man is worse than the first" (**Matt. 12:43-45b**). *"Stand fast therefore in the liberty by which Christ has made us free, and do not be entangled again with a yoke of bondage"* (**Gal. 5:1**).

When someone has been set free from demonic oppression, the same evil spirits will attempt re-entry. The person will face temptation in the areas where he was previously bound as the demons try to regain a foothold there. If the spirits see that the person is filled with Jesus and the Holy Spirit, they will know that they are unwelcome and unwanted. (The same sin patterns would allow them to feel at home again in that person.)

After you have ministered deliverance to someone, strongly suggest the following guidelines to help him retain his freedom:

1. Forgive those who hurt or offend you. Forgiving quickly will prevent a root of bitterness from developing. Refusing to forgive gives evil spirits a legal right of access.

2. Pursue peace with others. Attempt to walk in love, unity, and wisdom in relationships.

3. Spend time in God's Word. The Bible cleanses our souls from the contamination of the world; it renews our minds. (*see* **John 15:3**). Form a strategy for reading and studying it. Keep a journal of what the Lord says or highlights to you every day. *"Thus speaks the Lord God of Israel, saying: 'Write in a book for yourself all the words that I have spoken to you'"* (**Jer. 30:2**).

4. Guard your thought-life. The mind is a battleground; if you can win the battle in your mind, you can win it in your words and actions. Beware of the accusations of the devil against God, yourself, and others. Resist him; don't sin with your mind! *"Finally, brethren, whatever things are true, whatever things are noble, whatever things are just, whatever things are pure, whatever things are lovely, whatever things are of good report, if there is any virtue and if there is anything praiseworthy—meditate on these things"* (**Phil. 4:8**).

5. Resist temptation. Don't yield to temptation; rebuke the enemy immediately! Bring carnal desires and lusts to the cross. Repetitious sinning allows the enemy to oppress you.

6. Abide in Jesus. Be aware of His presence throughout the day. Stay intimately connected to the Lord; speak often with the Holy Spirit.

7. Fill your life with prayer and praise. Prayer, praise, and worship leave no room for evil spirits.

8. Meet regularly with believers. Attend a Bible-believing congregation and/or a small cell group or Bible study where personal nurturing is provided. Place yourself under godly authority for protection and accountability. *"And let us consider one another in order to stir up love and good works, not forsaking the assembling of ourselves together, as is the manner of some, but exhorting one another, and so much the more as you see the Day approaching"* (**Heb. 10:24-25**).

TWENTY-THREE

Freedom from Intimidation

"Listen to Me, you who know righteousness, you people in whose heart is My law: do not fear the reproach of men, nor be afraid of their revilings... I, even I, am He who comforts you. Who are you that you should be afraid of a man who will die, and of the son of a man who will be made like grass? And you forget the Lord your Maker, Who stretched out the heavens and laid the foundations of the earth..." (**Isa. 51:7, 12-13a**). *"Therefore I remind you to stir up the gift of God which is in you through the laying on of my hands. For God has not given us a spirit of fear, but of power and of love and of a sound mind"* (**2 Tim. 1:6-7**).

God has given each of us gifts, which we are to use assertively and authoritatively. **1 Timothy 4:14a** says, *"Do not neglect the gift that is in you..."* To neglect means to despise, underestimate, disregard, or ignore. These words speak of a lack of action, decisiveness, and authority. It is a serious thing to neglect what is entrusted to us by God. The main reason we do not use our God-given gifts is because of fear, or more literally, *intimidation.* The spirit of intimidation tries to keep us from doing what God has called us to do. It operates in the realm of the spirit, and we experience it in our soul. It causes us to compromise what we know to be right and to tolerate what we know to be wrong. Just as it was active in Paul and Timothy's day, so it is active in ours. We need to recognize this spirit so that we can deal effectively with it and get on with God's work.

Recognizing a Spirit of Intimidation

When a spirit of intimidation is oppressing us, we may feel overwhelmed with inferiority and fear. We feel depressed, confused, and inadequate. We battle worthlessness, and question God's call on our lives. This spirit unleashes discouragement and frustration, robbing us of proper perspective. Things we face may seem impossible. We imagine failure or ridicule. The stronger the intimidation, the more hopeless we feel.

The spirit of intimidation often attacks us after we have done a good work for the Lord. It attacked the prophet Elijah after he killed the false prophets of Baal and turned Israel back to God. In 1 Kings 19, we read that Elijah ran for his life. Discouraged and depressed, he felt alone and wanted to die. This spirit was after him through Queen Jezebel.

We need to be aware of the spirit realm so that we can recognize what is really going on. Without spiritual discernment, we will focus attention only on the feelings we have and not deal with the cause of those feelings. Since intimidation is a spirit, it cannot be fought on the level of our intellect or will. Having a positive mental attitude cannot overcome the attacks by this spirit. Spiritual resistance requires spiritual assistance (*see* **2 Cor. 10:3-5**). People who live in countries or cities over which there are ruling territorial spirits of control and intimidation are more vulnerable to attacks from this spirit.

The devil is always the author of intimidation and fear. His goal is to control and limit you. He might whisper lies directly to you, or he may work through people. When someone asked something of you and you agreed to it in order to maintain peace, you compromised because you were intimidated. If you recognize this spirit operating through a person, don't resist the person, but wisely refuse to be intimidated. Those who intimidate you will control you.

Roots of Intimidation

Fear will cause you to focus on yourself, which makes you vulnerable to intimidation. Perfect love casts out fear because love puts the focus on God and others rather than on self (**1 John 4:17-18**). The root of fear is the love of self. When you love your life, you try to save it. You are intimidated by anything that threatens it. A threatened person honors what he fears more than he honors God.

When we fear man, we feel anxious and suspicious, and we try to avoid rejection and confrontation. We are so busy protecting ourselves and serving men that we are ineffective in our service for God. Afraid of what man can do to us, we fail to give God what He deserves. We surrender our God-given authority.

Leaders who fear men will give people what they want rather than what they need. When they make decisions in order to be popular with others, they are motivated by intimidation. Their actions are not rooted in love for people but in love for themselves. When their decisions are resisted and they give in to the resistance, they've given away their authority. But if they refuse to be intimidated and choose to obey the Spirit of God, they will maintain their spiritual authority and the anointing with it.

Fearing God Dislodges Fear of Man

The only way to be free from intimidation is to walk in the fear of the Lord. The Bible says, *"In the fear of the Lord there is strong confidence"* (**Prov. 14:26a**). To fear God is to respect and revere Him, and give Him glory, honor, and praise. It is to esteem Him and His desires above our own. Those who fear God will not be afraid of man. They will care more about what God thinks than what men think. The fear of man will cause us to avoid rejection, harm, and reproach at all costs without considering God's rejection. It is to offend the One we cannot see in order not to offend those we *can* see. When we allow fear to dominate our hearts, we will lose our peace, courage, and security.

The fear of the Lord produces confidence and boldness, exactly what we need to get free from intimidation. We cannot focus on serving the Lord *and* pleasing people. *"For do I now persuade men, or God? Or do I seek to please men? For if I still pleased men, I would not be a bondservant of Christ"* (**Gal. 1:10**).

Boldness Is Empowered by a Holy Life

When we compromise our integrity through sin or pleasing people, we lay down our confidence in God. But when we're walking upright before Him, obeying His voice, and using our spiritual gifts, we can be bold. Boldness comes from walking in the three specific virtues that we see in 2 Timothy 1:7. It is not just *one* of these virtues but the combination of all three that we need.

Power—the power of the Holy Spirit and our God-given authority
Love—strong love for God that outweighs love for self and the need for man's approval
A sound mind—knowing God's character of faithfulness and love, and listening for His instructions, ready to obey Him

When we hear the Lord speak to us, we feel fresh faith and courage. We speak and act with confidence. We carry His authority. We love deeply and sacrificially. We are settled in our minds because we know His Word and will.

To Break Intimidation:

1. Pursue a pure heart before God. Deal with all anger, resentment, and lust.
2. Repent of yielding to intimidation and disobeying God.
3. Ask the Lord to stir up holy boldness and awaken His dormant gifts in you.
4. Resist the spirit of fear/intimidation in Jesus' name. Memorize the Scriptures used in this chapter as ammunition against the enemy when he tries to intimidate you.

Suggested Prayer

"Father, please expose and remove any insecurities in my life that have given a spirit of intimidation a place to attack me. Please heal any wounds that would cause me to yield to pleasing people and to a need for man's approval. Please meet my needs for love and acceptance. Purify my heart; cleanse me from all sin.

"I repent for allowing others to control me, and for yielding to fear. I'm sorry for disobeying You. I repent for neglecting the spiritual gifts and leadership You entrusted to me. Today I confess and renounce fear. I rebuke every spirit of intimidation; leave me in Jesus' name! I nullify all words of control and intimidation spoken over my life. I break the fear of man off of me in Jesus' name. I submit to God, and I resist every spirit of fear.

"I command every national spirit of intimidation and control to leave me in Jesus' name! I belong to the kingdom of God and will be ruled by the Lord Jesus and not by the spirit over _______ (name the nation). *I am under the Lord's reign! Lord Jesus, sit on the throne of my heart and rule me from within.*

"Father, please awaken in me the gifts You gave me. Stir up holy boldness in me. Baptize me in Your power and love, and give me a sound mind. I ask for an increase in all of these areas: more power in Your Holy Spirit, more love for God and others, and more soundness in my thinking and understanding of what You are saying to me. Thank You! In the name of Jesus, my Lord, amen."

Conclusion

As you walk with the Lord, take care not to allow previous failures to hold you back. Do not judge your future by where you've been. If you do, you'll never get beyond your past. God specializes in turning cowards into champions!

May you find complete freedom from all fear of man and be filled with a compelling love for God and holy boldness.

"The Lord is my light and my salvation; whom shall I fear? The Lord is the strength of my life; of whom shall I be afraid?" **(Ps. 27:1)**

TWENTY-FOUR

Healing for Heart Disease

"This is the genealogy of Terah: Terah begot Abram, Nahor, and Haran. Haran begot Lot. And Haran died before his father Terah in his native land, in Ur of the Chaldeans... And Terah took his son Abram and his grandson Lot, the son of Haran, and his daughter-in-law Sarai, his son Abram's wife, and they went out with them from Ur of the Chaldeans to go to the land of Canaan; and they came to Haran and dwelt there. So the days of Terah were two hundred and five years, and Terah died in Haran" (**Gen. 11:27-28, 31-32**). *"Hope deferred makes the heart sick, but when the desire comes, it is a tree of life"* (**Prov. 13:12**).

What anguish and grief Terah must have felt as his youngest son died prematurely, perhaps even in his presence. Later, on their way to Canaan, Terah's family passed through a city with the same name as his son, Haran. Instead of continuing on to Canaan, the Scripture says Terah *"came to Haran and dwelt there."* Not only did Terah settle in Haran, he died there. Maybe it was a false sense of guilt that held him there; perhaps it was unresolved grief. Whatever the reason, it appears that Terah was never able to truly live beyond Haran's death.

Longing for and grieving a deceased loved one is normal, but there comes a time when we need to move on. When we grieve for too long, the sorrow can give a spirit of heaviness an open door to oppress our soul. This evil spirit tries to diminish our hope and crush our joy; it breathes rejection, insecurity, and fear into us. We may embrace a false loyalty. We become stuck, unable to move forward to fulfill our God-given destiny.

With God's grace and help, we must choose to journey on to our "Canaan," or we, too, will die in Haran. We cannot permit the pain or disappointment of our past to rob us of what God has for us in the future. Losing a loved one is only one of the many causes of a broken heart. There are numerous other circumstances that threaten our joy and hope and result in a weak heart.

Some Causes of Disappointment (a sick heart)

- the death of a loved one or a lost destiny
- a failed marriage or failed business
- never having had the opportunity to marry
- health that was taken by sickness, disease, or an accident
- a broken promise, betrayal, or false accusation
- rejection, abandonment, and criticism from others
- a brave fight of faith that was seemingly lost
- unfulfilled or shattered hopes and dreams
- not having a second chance to make something right
- personal or moral failure

If your heart aches when you think about an unrealized dream, if your passion has waned and you have grown apathetic, your hope is deferred and your heart is sick. If you find yourself going through religious motions, doing and saying the right things while feeling empty and lifeless on the inside, you may be a victim of sustained grief. If tears come to your eyes when you think about a certain person; if disappointment seems stronger than your joy; if you cannot go to some places in your mind without pain; if a dream sparks disillusionment or cynicism instead of faith; if the statement *"God is going to come through for you"* is met with doubt, then you are in some stage of heart disease.

Reader's Digest reported that people with serious depression were three times more likely to die of heart disease. Even people with mild depression had a fatality rate 50% higher than normal. The loss of hope is crippling. It robs us of the will to live and causes our souls to be downcast. Having our hope deferred doesn't make us bad, weak, or unspiritual; it shows that we are human. Every one of us will fight spiritual heart disease a number of times in our lives.

Stages of Heart Disease

1. discouragement — the loss of courage, usually due to a failure or disappointment
2. confusion — questioning oneself, God, and one's dreams

3. unbelief — hope and expectations leave, and skepticism enters
4. disillusionment — questioning God's character
5. bitterness — deeply resentful; blaming God, others, or oneself
6. cynicism — a complete loss of faith and hope

King David had to battle against discouragement; he knew it could potentially destroy him. Three times in Psalm 42 he wrote about taking authority over his soul in order to win the battle in his heart. *"Why are you cast down, O my soul? And why are you disquieted within me? Hope in God; for I shall yet praise Him, the help of my countenance and my God"* (**Ps. 42:11**).

USA Statistics

- The divorce rate has risen over 279% in the last 27 years.
- 2.5 million people divorce every year.
- One million children are affected by divorce each year.
- Fatherless homes account for 63% of youth suicides, 90% of runaways, and 85% of youths in prison.
- The leading cause of disability is major depressive disorder. 19 million adults have a depressive disorder.
- The youth suicide rate has tripled in the past 35 years and is the #3 cause of death of those between the ages of 15-24.
- 25% of high school students consider suicide each year.
- 25% of all hospital admission is for psychiatric help.
- 70% of pastors constantly fight depression.
- 80% of adult children of pastors seek professional help for depression.

Are you a victim *of* or a victor *over* your sick heart? Tell your heart to take hope! Speak aloud to your soul! (e.g., *"Soul, hope in God! He will not fail you."*) *"This I recall to my mind, therefore I have hope... 'The Lord is my portion,' says my soul, 'Therefore I hope in Him' "* (**Lam. 3:21, 24**).

You may be weighed down with moral failure and regret, tragedy or deep grief, but Jesus wants to heal you. Where you have known sorrow and heaviness, He wants to give you *"beauty for ashes, the oil of joy for mourning, the garment of praise for the spirit of heaviness"* **(Isa. 61:3)**. Jesus is as anointed today as He was centuries ago to heal the brokenhearted. Nothing can heal your sick heart like Jesus can. He can restore your hope and joy. In **Luke 4:18**, He said, *"The Spirit of the Lord is upon Me, because He has anointed Me to preach the gospel to the poor; He has sent Me to heal the brokenhearted, to proclaim liberty to the captives and recovery of sight to the blind."*

In the scene of your deepest wounds or worst failures, the Lord offers you hope. God wants you to learn from your mistakes, but not to be held captive by them. Jesus came to deliver and restore you! He wants you to hope in His mercy and trust in His faithfulness. He wants to give you new vision. **Psalm 39:7** says, *"And now, Lord, what do I wait for? My hope is in You."* **Psalm 31:24** says, *"Be of good courage, and He shall strengthen your heart, all you who hope in the Lord."*

Suggested Prayer

"Father, I don't want to die in Haran, tied to grief and sentiment, tethered to __________'s tombstone or to my own failure of ___________. I want to move on and fulfill my calling. I want to reach my destiny, not just get halfway there. I've carried this ________ (death, grief, regret, trauma, failure, disappointment…) *within me long enough. I want freedom! Today, I bring to You my sick heart and deferred hope. Please restore hope and joy to me. Thank You for binding up my heart, for giving me beauty in place of ashes and the oil of joy for mourning. I resist the spirit of heaviness in the name of Jesus! I put on the garment of praise! Thank You, Jesus, for proclaiming liberty to me!"*

"Now may the God of hope fill you with all joy and peace in believing, that you may abound in hope by the power of the Holy Spirit" (**Rom. 15:13**).

TWENTY-FIVE

Healing Inner Wounds

"The Spirit of the Lord is upon Me, because He has anointed Me to preach the gospel to the poor; He has sent Me to heal the brokenhearted, to proclaim liberty to the captives and recovery of sight to the blind, to set at liberty those who are oppressed; to proclaim the acceptable year of the Lord" **(Luke 4:18-19)**.

We live in an imperfect world with imperfect people, and getting hurt in the process of trying to successfully maneuver through life is just part of the package. We have all been wounded. Some have been hurt much more than others, but *all* of us have experienced rejection and hurt to some degree. One psychologist said, *"It takes 18 years to become what we are; for the next 80 years we are being healed of it!"*

There are three things that we can do with the pain of our past. We can *regret* it, which leads to guilt and later to frustration and anger. Nothing chains a person to past failure like regret. We can *repeat* it, which leads to grief and becomes a cycle in our lives (e.g., divorce). Or we can *release* it, allowing God's grace to free us from shame and the recurrence of that failure or sin pattern.

A deep sorrow, disappointment, or grief can crush one's soul, devastating hope and joy. The hurt can be so deep that it settles into one's spirit, even temporarily forgotten by the mind and memory. *"For I am poor and needy, and my heart is wounded within me"* **(Ps. 109:22)**. *"...by sorrow of the heart, the spirit is broken"* **(Prov. 15:13)**. *"The spirit of a man will sustain him in sickness, but who can bear a broken spirit?"* **(Prov. 18:14)**

Whether lodged in the conscious or subconscious mind, unhealed wounds strongly influence us. Psychologists say we use up to 50% of our mental and emotional energy dealing with unresolved issues and inner pain. We express the pain through our behaviors, emotional responses, reactions, and choices.

Wounds in the soul drain us of energy, strength, and initiative. As long as we are holding onto inner pain, we are not free. We are enslaved by our hurts and damaged emotions. We live brokenly and ineffectively, seldom experiencing real joy and peace.

Wounded people tend to act in the present in response to the pain of their past whether or not they are aware of it. Consider the analogy of a smooth lake that appears clean on the surface, but on the bottom of the lake are broken bottles and cans coated with rust. The water looks pure, but it's terribly polluted. In the same way, on the surface we may look fine and smell sweet, but the hurts in our lives contaminate us. Rather than living water flowing from us, we often serve liquid woundedness. *"...out of the abundance of the heart the mouth speaks. A good man out of the good treasure of his heart brings forth good things, and an evil man out of the evil treasure brings forth evil things"* (**Matt. 12:34b-35**).

In order for the past not to determine our present and future, we need to forgive anyone who hurt us and allow the Lord to do a deep work of cleansing and healing in our hearts. Part of our inner transformation and corresponding outward holiness is directly linked to allowing the Lord to minister to us deep within. The Lord wants to heal the areas of our personalities that come short of His glory. The work of atonement that Jesus accomplished on the cross is sufficient for all of our sin and inner pain. When He sets us free, we are free indeed!

Some of you who feel called to counsel are carrying wounds in your souls that you haven't allowed the Lord to heal. Each of us needs to seek healing from Jesus so that we can minister to others freely without preoccupation and projection. We must pursue wholeness so that we can be effective vessels of His mercy and restoration.

What Causes Inner Wounds?

1. Most wounds are caused by rejection, ill treatment, or abuse. The sin may be intentional or unintentional. The most common abuses are physical, verbal, emotional, sexual, abandonment/neglect, religious, and shame.

2. Wounds can come from traumatic events, such as fires, accidents, the death of loved ones, and divorce. The trauma wounds the inner man and becomes a part of who he or she is in the future.

3. Some wounds are self-inflicted. The pain or grief we have caused others—intentional or not—can deeply damage *us*. We may reject and hate ourselves. Examples of these wounds are acts of immorality, abortion, violence or vandalism, and accidentally hurting (or killing) someone.

Common Signs of Inner Wounds

1. A deep sense of unworthiness is manifested by feelings of anxiety, inadequacy, and inferiority. The hurt has gone so deep that it has drained one's self-esteem. Her self-talk may be: *"I'm a loser. I can't do anything right. I'm not worthy of love."*

2. Insecurity is feeling unsafe and helpless. The insecure fear trusting people, so they cling to and smother those they *do* trust. Children who grow up without the *expressed* love of a father often have deep-seated insecurities.

3. Perfectionism is compulsively striving to achieve perfect performance. Striving for perfection is often a reaction to being rejected due to past failure; the wound is so painful that the person avoids future failure at all costs. The perfectionist lives a driven life. He may work hard to earn God's love; he cannot believe in and receive His grace. Or he might quit trying to please, be tidy, or make high grades because he fears failure. His attitude is, *"If I can't do it right, I won't do it at all."*

4. Super-sensitivity causes a person to live with a continual sense of rejection; he is easily offended. We feel we must "walk on eggshells" around him in order not to upset him.

5. "Emotionally incapacitated" describes a person who needs endless amounts of affection and affirmation. No amount of appreciation or praise is sufficient to fill their love deficit.

6. Depression is sadness and apathy caused by holding anger and wounds within. The combination of hurt and repressed anger does not simply go away. If it is not properly dealt with, it will eventually show up in a form of depression.

7. Sexual problems including deviancy, fear of intimacy, and distorted views of sexuality can be caused by rejection (especially rejection by the parent of the same gender), incest, promiscuity, sexual abuse, rape, and viewing pornographic materials.

8. Disease and illness can result from traumatic wounds to the soul. Doctors estimate that 75% of human illnesses are emotionally or psychologically based. Some headaches, ulcers, arthritis, and other inflammatory diseases can be linked to wounds from relationships.

9. Over-reactiveness is reacting way out of proportion to a person or situation. This is caused by a painful word or action touching an area where there has been previous hurt. It is like having a physical bruise that gets bumped; the skin is extra sensitive in that area (e.g., Pete was sensitive to criticism because he received an excessive amount of it as a teenager.).

10. Fear of additional rejection, hurt, and embarrassment keeps a person in bondage, preventing him from enjoying healthy relationships for fear of more pain. Expecting hurt and rejection so terrifies him that the fear itself is worse than the previous hurt.

11. Addictions to alcohol, drugs, immorality, sex, pornography, crime, food, TV, computers, video games, social networking, relationships, and exercise are a sign of pain-management. What may begin as a way to cope with pain can become a life-controlling problem.

The Lord wants to heal our inner wounds and transform our character flaws. **Psalm 147:3** says that God *"...heals the brokenhearted and binds up their wounds."* King David wrote in **Psalm 41:4**, *"...Lord, be merciful to me; Heal my soul, for I have sinned against You."*

Isaiah 53:5d says, *"...by His stripes we are healed."* Because Jesus *"is the same yesterday, today, and forever"* (**Heb. 13:8**), He can heal today what was wounded yesterday, last year, even 20 years ago!

Steps to Healing

1. Forgive from your heart everyone who has caused you pain. *"...we also forgive everyone who is indebted to us"* (**Luke 11:4**). If your wounds are caused by your own sinfulness, you need to request and receive God's forgiveness.

2. Renounce all strongholds of wrong thinking, lies and deception, and anything inconsistent with the true knowledge of God. Bring every thought captive to the obedience of Christ (*see* **2 Cor. 10:5b**). This includes lies about God, yourself, and others. Take care not to label people according to a previous offence, expecting them to repeat it.

3. Repent of self-pity, bitterness, and hope for revenge. Be willing to change behaviors, thought patterns, and how you relate to others. Do not let your comfort zone of unhappiness determine your destiny.

4. Be committed to loving and serving God. If you only seek to be relieved of pain, you may not find lasting healing. Progressive healing is vitally connected to an intimate relationship with God. Abiding in Him is a key to wholeness. Being unfaithful to the Lord can open the door for insecurities, fears, and strongholds to return.

5. Rely upon the power and grace of God to complete the work He has begun in you. Keep your eyes on the Lord, not on the counselor or yourself. Allow the Word of God to instruct you in putting off the old self and putting on the new (*see* **Eph. 4:21-32**).

Helping Someone Find Healing

Be compassionate and gentle as you get alongside others in their pursuit of wholeness. It is the Lord who heals, but you are His vessel of mercy and love. You must be sensitive and led by the Holy Spirit.

Pray specifically over hurtful events (even prenatal experiences if the Lord reveals trauma during that time; e.g., an attempted abortion). It may be necessary to loose the counselee from things, people, or places connected with the trauma. Ask the Lord to heal the person's soul from every painful event or damaged emotion. As the wound is healed, the emotions may surface again. But healing will follow, and the memory will lose its painfulness and fade in time.

Pray over specific memories and tormenting thoughts. Remind counselees to resist the enemy when he reminds them of things that have been put under Jesus' blood (their own sin or that of others) and to thank God for His cleansing and forgiveness.

The healing of wounds begins with prayer and continues as we walk with the Lord. Achieving wholeness is a lifelong process. Cultivating intimacy with the Lord Jesus and knowing God the Father's love is imperative! The healing may not be instant, but it will have begun, and it will continue.

"...He who has begun a good work in you will complete it until the day of Jesus Christ" (**Phil. 1:6b**). *"Now may the God of peace Himself sanctify you completely; and may your whole spirit, soul, and body be preserved blameless at the coming of our Lord Jesus Christ"* (**1 Thess. 5:23**).

TWENTY-SIX

A Healing Encounter with Jesus

"The Lord also will be a refuge for the oppressed, a refuge in times of trouble. And those who know Your name will put their trust in You; for You, Lord, have not forsaken those who seek You" **(Ps. 9:9-10)**.

As mentioned before, a definition of personality and the expression of outward character is how we perceive our past, experience our present, and anticipate our future. It is not so much our previous experiences that dictate to us, as it is our perception of them. We must see our past from God's redeeming perspective and let it thrust us onto Him, where we can receive His healing and restoration.

It is a blessing when we can receive prayer from a pastor, counselor, or trusted friend, but often we deal with our inner pain alone with God. These encounters are precious! Meeting with God over the most painful issues of our lives will result in greater attachment to and love for Him. We realize that only God can carry and sustain us; we trust Him all the more because of those significant times where He leaves His fingerprints on our souls. When you realize that you need (further) inner healing, make an appointment with the Lord where you will not be distracted or disrupted. Then pray through the following steps and stages as thoroughly as you can.

1. Invite Jesus into the wounded areas of your heart. We often mishandle our brokenness. Because it hurts so much to deal with the pain, we repress our hurts and emotions. By doing this, we may find temporary relief, but we do not find lasting healing. Locked away inside of our hearts, the pain festers, contaminating our souls. Then it seeps out in our words, actions and reactions, defiling those around us. If we will face the reality that we need help, open the door of our hearts to Jesus, and allow Him to walk through the painful situations with us, we can find healing.

The Lord will never enter any area where we have placed "no trespassing" signs; He waits for our permission (*see* **Rev. 3:20**). So, the first step we need to take is to honestly talk about our hurts and disappointments with Him.

"Jesus, please enter the deep recesses of my heart and heal the wounds there. I'm weary from carrying this pain; I need Your help. I especially want to talk with You about __________. I'll do what I have to in order to be healed: I'll change my ways, confess my sin, forgive others, and risk trusting You at a deeper level. Whatever it takes, I'll do it! 'Create in me a clean heart, O God, and renew a steadfast spirit within me' (**Ps. 51:10**)*."*

2. Renounce agreements you have made with the messages of your wounds. All wounds give messages such as, *"You are worthless"* or *"You're a disappointment."* Because these messages are attached to intense pain, they feel true, so we accepted them as fact. We tend to make promises in our hearts that are connected with the messages. For example, *"Since I'm a failure, I won't attempt anything where I might fail."* To find healing, we must reject the messages of our wounds, believe God's truth, and renounce the promises we made to ourselves based on the lies we believed.

Write down the messages and lies you have believed and the promises you have made that have come from your hurts. Use your journal to do this. Here are some guidelines for you:

- Lies I have believed about God, about myself, or others:
- The truth (based on God's Word):
- Promises I have made because of hurts I received:

Now pray something like this: *"Father, I repent for believing lies about You, myself, and others; please forgive me. I renounce the agreements I made with the messages of rejection. I reject and renounce the lies. I choose to believe You. I believe that I am Your beloved child, and that You will care for me. I renounce the promises I made to myself that are damaging to others or me. I cancel them in Jesus' name! Please set me free to be who You want me to be and to fulfill my God-given destiny."*

3. Grieve the pain of the past. Grief is a form of validation. It says the wound mattered. Your feelings matter. What happened to you should not have happened. It is not the way life was supposed to be. We must bring closure to hurts in order to live emotionally mature as adults. Weep the unwept tears over your wounds and damaged emotions. Expressing grief is a necessary part of healing. Give yourself permission to feel emotions, including those of anger, remorse, and fear.

"Lord, I've suppressed my emotions for so long; please help me release them. Help me to feel the pain, so that I can forgive from the depths of my soul. Help me to grieve adequately and to release the past so that it doesn't control me anymore. Set my emotions free; heal and restore them as I express them now in Your presence. Thank You, Jesus."

4. Forgive those who hurt you. Feelings take time to heal after the choice of forgiveness is made. If your expression of forgiveness does not touch the emotional core of your life, it will be incomplete. Admit to yourself and to God that what happened or was said hurt you. Then choose to forgive.

Forgiveness says, *"What you did was wrong; it hurt me deeply, but I release you. I forgive the debt, and I entrust you to God. You owe me nothing."* It helps to remember that those who wounded you were hurting themselves and were used by the enemy to harm you. *"Let all bitterness, wrath, anger, clamor, and evil speaking be put away from you, with all malice... be kind to one another, tenderhearted, forgiving one another, even as God in Christ forgave you"* (**Eph. 4:31-32**).

"Father, I choose to forgive everyone who has hurt, disappointed, or offended me. I release every offense. I cancel the debts against me even as You cancelled my debt against You. I bless these people in Your name! Please pour out Your Spirit upon them. Heal their souls and bodies; strengthen their marriages and families. Bless their businesses and ministries. Thank You, Lord."

5. Ask Jesus to comfort you. Let the Lord take you into His comforting arms and heal your pain. Invite Him into each trauma you experienced. Spend time in His presence, allowing Him to flood you with His life, peace, and healing.

*"Jesus, please heal my heart. Touch the shattered places in my soul. Hold the wounded child within me. Set me free from the effects of __________ (name the pain, sin, or trauma). Free me from captivity to the enemy and to pain. Release me from all darkness. Heal my soul. 'Restore to me the joy of Your salvation, and uphold me by Your generous Spirit' (**Ps. 51:12**). In all places of destruction and death within me, please release Your life. I receive Your healing touch, and I thank You for it."*

6. Let God parent you. *"When my father and my mother forsake me, the Lord will take care of me" (**Ps. 27:10**).* There is a central part of your heart that was made for God and His unconditional love. You will never be able to find this love in human relationships. Only God can fill your love deficit. Ask Him to overwhelm your heart with His love. *"For you did not receive the spirit of bondage again to fear, but you received the Spirit of adoption by whom we cry out, 'Abba, Father' "* (**Rom. 8:15**).

Father, I need You. Please pour Your love into the depths of my heart. Reveal to me who You really are; correct my distorted perceptions of You. Parent me! Give me fresh revelation of You as my Father! I receive Your love. Thank You, Abba."

7. Stand and lift your hands to God in worship. By doing this, you are symbolically putting the pain and the past under your feet and turning your focus and expectation onto Him Who loves you with an eternal love. Praise and adore Him. As the Lord inhabits your praises (**Ps. 22:3**), He will comfort you. Every place where your heart aches and where you have felt rejection and emptiness, He will fill with His indescribable love.

8. Ask God to give you a new way of looking at your old hurts. Don't try to come up with good reasons for why you suffered as you did. Let the *Lord* reveal the value of your pain to you. Ask Him to show you what you gained through what you lost. Rejoice in God's ability to make all things work together for good (**Rom. 8:28**). Then, change your "self-talk" (what you say to yourself).

Joseph is a good biblical example of how God can *"work all things together for good."* Everything that Joseph suffered would seem cruel and unfair except that the Lord was shaping him for His purposes. Although Joseph was rejected by his family and sold into slavery, falsely accused, punished and imprisoned for a crime he didn't commit, he never showed bitterness. He kept his heart clean toward God and worked hard with a good attitude even while a slave or in prison. We see his purity of heart when he said to his brothers who had severely mistreated him years earlier, *"But as for you, you meant evil against me; but God meant it for good..."* (**Gen. 50:20**). Joseph acknowledged that God was there all the time, allowing his trials. God intended Joseph's suffering to develop him into a man whom He could trust with authority and power. And it did! When Joseph was ready, God suddenly promoted him to a ruling position in Egypt where he was able to save the Hebrew race from extinction.

"Joseph called the name of his firstborn Manasseh: 'For God has made me forget all my toil and all my father's house' " (**Gen. 41:51**). God caused Joseph to forget the difficulty and pain he had experienced. *"And the name of the second he called Ephraim: 'For God has caused me to be fruitful in the land of my affliction' "* (**Gen. 41:52**). God made Joseph fruitful in the place where he was previously afflicted and enslaved.

God has not promised to keep us from pain and suffering, but He *has* promised to make us fruitful in the midst of it. Each of us will pass through valleys before we reach our final destination, and God will use all that for future plans that only He knows. As we remain faithful to the Lord in our trials, His nature will be worked into our lives. With Jesus as our Lord, a time will come when God will enable us to forget the troubles of our past. He will make us fruitful in the land of our affliction, and while our hearts are satisfied and God is glorified, many people will be touched by what God produces in us.

God does not waste our trials; He uses them to transform us into His image and to release His love, power, and healing to those around us. He knows that our lives—what we are through His grace—will help others find God's victory in their lives.

The Lord intends to use us to unlock God's destiny for others. So, throw yourself on the altar and let God break you… and heal you. Allow Him to make you broken bread and poured-out wine to minister His life to a wounded and dying world.

"Lord, help me to remember that the crises I experience always precede Your enrichment in my life. You DO overcome evil with good! I understand that the place of fruitfulness is often in the land of affliction, so I surrender to You again today in THIS place. Jesus, be glorified in me. May I be a magnet to draw others to You no matter what I am going through. For the glory of Your name, amen."

9. Spend time thanking God for your new perspective. Let God show you your life with His purposes in mind. Your old outlook was there for a long time, and your new perspective may need some time to take root. Let it transform your thoughts, beliefs, and emotions.

"Thank You for redeeming the conflicts and pain of my life. Your faithfulness is my refuge. Thank You for healing me and causing me to forget the trauma of my past. My future is bright in You; I have fresh hope! Please cement into my thoughts and beliefs this new perspective that You have given me. I bless Your name, Jesus!"

"Bless the Lord, O my soul; and all that is within me, bless His holy name!... Who redeems your life from destruction, who crowns you with lovingkindness and tender mercies" **(Ps. 103:1, 4)**.

TWENTY-SEVEN

Sanctified Soul Ties

" 'And you shall love the Lord your God with all your heart, with all your soul, with all your mind, and with all your strength.' This is the first commandment. And the second, like it, is this: 'You shall love your neighbor as yourself.' There is no other commandment greater than these" (**Mark 12:30-31**). *"Now when he had finished speaking to Saul, the soul of Jonathan was knit to the soul of David, and Jonathan loved him as his own soul...Then Jonathan and David made a covenant, because he loved him as his own soul. And Jonathan took off his robe that was on him and gave it to David, with his armor; even to his sword and his bow and his belt"* (**1 Sam. 18:1, 3-4**).

The first and greatest commandment is to love God with all of our hearts, souls, minds, and strength. Jesus is to be our foremost love, the One Who captivates our hearts and holds them close to His own.

Basilea Schlink, in her book, *Those Who Love Him*, describes first love this way:

"First love" is first-class love, that of greatest quality. This love has eyes for the bridegroom alone. He fills her every thought, her every moment; to Him goes the yearning of her heart. Bridal love is a lavish love...a sacrificial love, giving everything to the Beloved. Compared to the Beloved, all else is empty and worthless. Bridal love has one dominant characteristic: it occupies itself exclusively with Jesus, is always available to Him, and finds complete fulfillment in Him.

God is jealous for our adoration and devotion. He deserves first place in our hearts and is satisfied with nothing less. Loving Him with all that we are frees us from unhealthy attractions to this world or to unholy entanglements in human relationships. Soul ties can be good, as in marriage or a covenant friendship like David and Jonathan shared. But a soul tie can also be destructive. It must then be severed so that we can bond appropriately to Jesus and to those with whom soul ties are acceptable. Having a soul tie means one's thoughts, emotions, and actions are governed by a particular relationship.

Instead of one's heart belonging solely to Jesus and being under His lordship, that person is held captive to do the will of another. Voluntary soul ties are formed when one idolizes someone or something. Involuntary captivity means one is held captive against their will, such as in human trafficking, child abuse, or enmeshed family relationships.

Although sometimes we are in bondage to things and places, most of our attachments are with people. When we are controlled emotionally, we feel scattered, indecisive and confused, and are unable to fully enjoy other relationships. When the ongoing presence and nurturing of a particular person is necessary for our happiness, we have an emotional dependency on him/her. When our worth, peace of mind, inner stability, and security are anchored on a person and their response to us, we are emotionally dependent. Emotionally dependent relationships are usually held together through control and manipulative tactics.

Signs of Emotional Dependency

You know you are emotionally dependent when you...

- are jealous and possessive with your friend
- prefer to spend time alone with one friend and feel frustrated when you see him/her only in groups or with others present
- feel irrationally angry or depressed when your friend withdraws
- find other relationships boring compared to this one
- experience romantic or sexual feelings leading to fantasy about them
- are preoccupied with their appearance, personality, and problems
- refuse to make short or long-term plans that do not include them
- are unable to see his/her faults realistically
- are physically affectionate beyond what is appropriate
- feel you cannot survive without that person
- refer frequently to them in conversation or feel free to speak for them
- exhibit an intimacy or familiarity with your friend that causes others to feel embarrassed or uncomfortable in your presence

Manipulation to Establish and Maintain Dependent Relationships

- wearing each other's clothing and copying one another's styles
- using poetry or music to provoke an emotional response
- staring at each other or giving meaningful or seductive looks

- refusing to make eye contact as a means of punishment
- flattering, flirting, teasing, and/or using special nicknames
- expressing inappropriate or excessive physical affection
- giving cards and gifts regularly to him or her for no special reason
- making the other person feel guilty over unmet expectations
- keeping the other's time occupied so as not to allow for separate, independent activities.

Codependent Relationships

Codependency, similar to emotional dependency, is a fruit of rejection and a form of "relationship addiction." Codependency is mutual whereas emotional dependency can be one-way. The need to be loved, accepted, and needed causes a person to attach himself to someone. The root sin of codependency is idolatry; it is allowing someone other than Jesus to control one's life or be their life-source.

Codependent people depend on others in the ways they should depend on the Lord. They insist on being in control, feel insecure and vulnerable, and are unaware of the sin and deception of the addiction. Codependents suppress their own emotions and deny their own identity in favor of the one they love. Their need to relate to and be with the other is intense. They seek to please so that they don't offend or lose them. They refuse to make decisions without consulting one another. They have virtually no boundaries with their friend. Possessiveness and jealousy are a natural part of the relationship.

Other Types of Inappropriate Bonding

Immoral relationships. All sexual relationships create soul ties. To break that tie, a person will need to repent and forsake the sin, ask the Lord for forgiveness and cleansing, sincerely renounce the immorality, and verbally sever the soul tie(s) (naming each person involved) in the name of Jesus Christ.

Enmeshed relationships within a family. Enmeshed family relationships are commonly caused by (1) dominant authority figures in the family who control the other family members, (2) emotionally weak and dependent parents who live vicariously through their children, or (3) a parent who refuses to allow his children to become vocationally what they want to be by suppressing their growth or holding them in emotional bondage.

Even as adults, such children remain immature. To reach emotional maturity and to fulfill their destiny, they need to sever the entanglements through prayer and place proper boundaries in the relationships.

An abusive parent. Victims of sexual abuse have soul ties with their abuser(s). Romantic or hateful feelings are directed toward the one(s) who abused them. Strong feelings toward a parent—positive or negative—can block the flow of normal feelings for a spouse.

Parents are considered abusive when they give parental authority and responsibility to a child who is too young for it. When children are in the position of rearing other children, they can form unhealthy, unnatural parental bonds with those they parent. These bonds stimulate over-responsibility, which may cause them difficulty in relating correctly to others later.

When children become substitutes for spouses, they develop an adult-to-adult relationship with the parent rather than the proper child-to-adult relationship. Emotional incest occurs when a parent looks to a child for emotional support. Sexually abused children may live in a fantasy, unable to admit to the hurt and damage they've experienced. They cover for the abuser, often taking the blame for the ill treatment they received.

Bondages Not Directly Linked to Persons

Institutions and organizations. When an institution or organization becomes our reason for living and the recipient of our devotion, we have bonded inappropriately. These bonds are common with cults, businesses, the military, or congregations.

Unresolved grief, anger, or abandonment. Sometimes the soul tie we have is not linked to a current relationship, but to a person from our past. Unexpressed and unresolved grief or anger from past experiences can keep us in emotional turmoil for years. After sufficient grieving, we need to surrender the pain to Jesus and leave the past behind.

Jesus Provides Freedom

When we are emotionally dependent or codependent, we need to repent of idolatry and ask God to forgive us. Following our confession, we must ask Him to sever the bonds that are inappropriate, to integrate us within, and to unite our divided hearts. *"Teach me Your way, O Lord; I will walk in Your truth; unite my heart to fear Your name"* (**Ps. 86:11**).

Once Jesus sets us free from unhealthy entanglements, we can focus more fully on Him. The healing that follows may take months and require us to severely limit our interactions with former friends. Just as an alcoholic has to avoid alcohol while he is breaking the addiction, so when we break addictions to people, we need to avoid them for a while and concentrate on making Jesus the center of our lives.

Practical Steps to Freedom

1. Repent of idolatry, naming the person(s) or thing to which you have bonded. In repentance, you turn *from* the sin *to* the Lord. Repent of bonding inappropriately and renounce the bondage. Establish the Lord Jesus on the throne of your heart (again).

2. Ask God to sever the negative soul tie and to release you and the other person from it.

3. Forgive from your heart everyone who has abused or controlled you. Dispose of the possessions that connected you to those with whom you had wrong ties (jewelry, gifts, photographs, letters). If the bondage is to material things, ask the Spirit to show you what to throw away or burn.

4. Ask the Lord to heal and unite your heart, bringing the dispersed pieces together again. Ask Him to bond your heart to His. Healing takes time, but as you read God's Word and allow it to renew your mind and restore your heart, you will heal more quickly. *"He sent His word and healed them, and delivered them from their destructions"* (**Ps. 107:20**).

Having an intimate relationship with God is fundamental to your healing. Because humans are prone to addiction, it is vital that you develop an addiction to *the Lord*, so that you do not exchange an unhealthy bondage for another. Also, ask the Lord to bond you with those people in your life with whom it is appropriate, like spouses and children.

Suggested Prayer

"Lord God, I confess my sin of idolatry. I have formed unhealthy soul ties. Instead of bonding to You, I have given my devotion and worship to others. I have let them control my life. Please forgive me. Deliver me of idolatry; I repent of it and renounce it in Jesus' name! Lord Jesus, please sever all of my inappropriate ties with others. Release _______ and me from this bondage. Please break any and every improper soul tie that captures my thoughts and emotions, and draws me from You or from my lawful significant relationships. Unite my heart to fear Your name. Bond me to You and to those with whom soul ties are appropriate. Amen."

Believe you are free based on **1 John 1:9**, *"If we confess our sins, He is faithful and righteous to forgive us our sins and to cleanse us from all unrighteousness."* Once you are free from codependency and inappropriate soul ties, make every effort to stay free! *"O Lord our God, masters besides You have had dominion over us; but by You only we make mention of Your name"* (**Isa. 26:13**). Make Jesus lord of all of your relationships. Become established in God and actively pursue a deeper bond with Him.

Bonding with Jesus

1. Spend time in the Scriptures. The Word of God cleanses our souls (mind, will, and emotions) from the contamination of the world. Let the Word renew your mind and align it with the thoughts and purposes of God. Grow in your knowledge of the Lord by reading the Bible. From the Scriptures, we get a correct perception of God, and the distortions or lies we have believed are corrected with truth. *"This Book of the Law shall not depart from your mouth, but you shall meditate in it day and night, that you may observe to do according to all that is written in it. For then you will make your way prosperous, and then you will have good success"* (**Josh. 1:8**).

2. Fellowship with the Lord throughout the day. Besides cultivating a continual awareness of Jesus, make time in your schedule to give God your undivided attention. Make it a priority to listen to Him as well as to pour out your heart in prayer. Intimacy with the Lord is very important in the bonding process. We grow in our love for those with whom we have rich and intimate fellowship. *"Pray without ceasing"* (**1 Thess. 5:17**).

3. Praise and worship the Lord often. Thanksgiving and praise keep our focus on Jesus and prevent us from falling into self-pity and discontent. Sometimes it is not a lack of prayer, but a lack of *praise* that is our downfall. The book of Psalms is full of the praises of God; use them as a springboard for your expressions of worship to Him. *"Praise the Lord! Praise, O servants of the Lord. Praise the name of the Lord! Blessed be the name of the Lord from this time forth and forevermore! From the rising of the sun to its going down the Lord's name is to be praised"* (**Ps. 113:1-3**).

4. Guard your thoughts. Take special care to protect your mind from idolatrous thoughts of others and from negative, bitter thoughts. Avoid anything (pictures, TV, the Internet, music) that feeds sensual curiosity or lust. Make sure your thoughts are pleasing to the Lord.

In order to become like Jesus, we need a renewed mind! If we can get our thinking right, our actions and feelings will follow. God wants our thoughts and ways to line up with His.

Pray this verse often: *"Let the words of my mouth and the meditation of my heart be acceptable in Your sight, O Lord, my strength and my Redeemer"* (**Ps. 19:14**).

5. Abide in Jesus; try to please Him always. To abide means to camp out or to endure. To abide in Jesus means to pitch a tent in Him and live there! In our determination to please God, we will abhor evil (and addictions and wrong soul ties), and we will love and fear Him. *"Abide in Me, and I in you. As the branch cannot bear fruit of itself, unless it abides in the vine, so neither can you, unless you abide in Me. I am the vine, you are the branches; he who abides in Me, and I in him, he bears much fruit; for apart from Me you can do nothing"* (**John 15:4-5**).

Ask the Lord to choose good friends for you. Make Jesus lord of your relationships. If you feel a warning in your spirit about getting close to a particular person, listen to it! Obey the Holy Spirit! To ignore those checks could cause relational pain or temptation from which God wants to protect you. Pray, *"Lord, with whom do You want me to relate meaningfully? Please align me with the people of Your choice!"*

6. Run to the altar when you realize you are falling into bondage. When we realize we are headed toward unhealthy relationships, we need to *run* to the Lord. We have obviously neglected His presence too long! We must race to the prayer closet—our secret place with Him—and recapture our first love. Intimacy with Jesus and closely bonding with Him will prevent our hearts and minds from wandering to other people or things to satisfy us. *"Let us therefore draw near with confidence to the throne of grace, that we may receive mercy and may find grace to help in time of need"* (**Heb. 4:16**, NASB).

Most inappropriate soul ties are a result of trying to fill the love deficit inside. Only God's love can fill that void! When you are established in His love and have cultivated keen discernment, you can build healthy relationships that will be a blessing to Him, others, and yourself.

Characteristics of Healthy Friendships

Solid, healthy friendships…

- are based on shared experiences and growing trust. There is no safe way to rush this process.
- give life and joy; they do not take life. They are always loyal.
- allow for enjoyment of one another without the urge to possess or control.
- seldom contain jealousies over other friendships
- unselfishly promote growth, encouraging the other to realize their dreams.
- seldom examine or discuss the relationship, unless they experience a conflict. Much more time is spent focusing together on mutual interests or topics outside the friendship.
- hold no magnetic power over each other's thoughts or emotions.
- call forth the best in each other. Though they have times of being vulnerable, they don't try to keep each other in a weak place.

"Then Jonathan said to David, 'Go in peace, since we have both sworn in the name of the Lord, saying, "May the Lord be between you and me, and between your descendants and my descendants, forever…" ' " (**1 Sam. 20:42**).

TWENTY-EIGHT

Built on the True Foundation

"Now, therefore, you are no longer strangers and foreigners, but fellow citizens with the saints and members of the household of God, having been built on the foundation of the apostles and prophets, Jesus Christ Himself being the chief cornerstone, in whom the whole building, being fitted together, grows into a holy temple in the Lord, in whom you also are being built together for a dwelling place of God in the Spirit" (**Eph. 2:19-22**). *"For no other foundation can anyone lay than that which is laid, which is Jesus Christ"* (**1 Cor. 3:11**).

We are being built into a dwelling place for the Lord. What an awesome privilege and responsibility! For the Body of Messiah to be united and built together into a holy temple for God to inhabit, we must have a correct foundation. Jesus must be the chief cornerstone in our lives, and our foundation should be the teaching of the founding apostles and prophets.

Because our foundation is vitally important, the enemy targets that to derail us early in life. He tries to lay other foundations in our lives, such as fear, rejection and abandonment, anger and violence, pride, deception, lust, performance, and poverty. Even after surrendering to the Lord, we often live by the dictates of a faulty foundation rather than by God's Word. When our repentance is thorough, we receive some inner healing and deliverance, and we are intentionally discipled in God's Word, this does not pose such a problem. But because often we pray a "sinner's prayer" without true repentance and we receive little or no inner healing or Bible training, we try to build a new life with God on a shaky foundation.

"But why do you call Me 'Lord, Lord,' and not do the things which I say? Whoever comes to Me, and hears My sayings and does them [as an obedient disciple] ... *is like a man building a house, who dug deep* [repentance] *and laid the foundation* [Scripture] *on the rock* [Jesus]. *And when the flood arose, the stream beat vehemently against that house, and could not shake it, for it was founded on the rock.*

But he who heard and did nothing is like a man who built a house... without a foundation, against which the stream beat vehemently; and immediately it fell. And the ruin of that house was great" (**Luke 6:46-49**).

Uproot Faulty Foundations

Is Jesus the chief cornerstone of your life? Is scriptural teaching your foundation? If so, you will be able to withstand temptations and trials and emerge an overcomer. However, if you have only *added* Jesus to your life, and He isn't your center, you are in danger. If your life is not founded on God's Word, you will not be able to endure during difficult times. According to Jeremiah 1:10, we have to root out, pull down, destroy, and throw down before we can build and plant. So, we uproot and destroy faulty foundations by confessing family iniquity and repenting of sin. When wrong foundations are not removed and replaced, the enemy has access to tempt and torment us in those areas.

For instance, if a foundation of rejection and abandonment is laid in your life (maybe through abusive or neglectful authorities), then the enemy may torment you with fear of rejection and perceived rejection. The foundation of rejection draws further rejection *to* you from people. Initial abuse lays the foundation, and subsequent abuse builds on it. If the enemy laid a foundation of anger and violence in your life from the iniquity of your forefathers and/or from what you suffered as a child, then you are susceptible to temptations of anger and violence toward others, *and* the enemy draws anger and violence *to* you from others to build further on that foundation.

Each time you give into the sin of your defective foundation, or every time the enemy builds on that foundation through more of the same sins against you, the stronghold is more firmly entrenched in your life. The enemy lays layer upon layer on the foundation he initially laid, which further holds you in bondage. The good news is that our Almighty God can break up our flawed foundations and rebuild them with Jesus as the cornerstone! But we are not passive in this process. After asking the Lord to be the rock and cornerstone of our lives, we need to study the Scriptures to see how to live.

We need to line up our lives with God's Word. We replace lies with truth, unbelief with faith, and pride with humility. A foundation laid by Jesus will be solid. It will attract love and kindness (and persecution), even as our defective foundation attracted abuse and sin.

In **Hosea 2:19-20** God said, *"I will betroth you to Me forever; yes, I will betroth you to Me in righteousness and justice, in lovingkindness and mercy; I will betroth you to Me in faithfulness, and you shall know the Lord."* Although He said these words to Israel, they also apply to us in the New Covenant. A Hebrew betrothal is as binding as a marriage covenant. Notice that in each area where He betroths us to Himself, He replaces faulty foundations with a firm foundation:

- In place of rejection and abandonment, the Lord betroths us to Himself *forever*! We can be secure in knowing He never leaves us. Our covenant with Him is eternal.
- In place of pride and disobedience, the Lord lays a foundation of righteousness.
- In place of poverty, injustice, and abuse, the Lord rebuilds our foundation with justice.
- In place of performance and perfectionism, the Lord offers us grace.
- In place of anger, bitterness, and violence, the Lord provides us with mercy and peace.
- In place of unfaithfulness, lust, and deception, He lays a foundation of faithfulness.
- In place of fear and confusion, He promises that we will intimately know Him (and His love and truth).

As God renewed His covenant with Israel in these verses with wedding vows, so He promises us in the New Covenant a relationship characterized by permanence, security, right standards, fair treatment, unfailing love and devotion, tenderness, and an ongoing revelation of Himself. He wants to move us from a slave mentality into an intimate friendship with Him where we know we are loved and precious. *"...I will have mercy on her who had not obtained mercy; then I will say to those who were not My people, 'You are My people!' And they shall say, 'You are my God!'"* (**Hosea 2:23b**).

Use the following prayer to break up the flawed foundations of your life. Ask the Lord to establish His reign in you. Go beyond this written prayer to freely express your heart to God.

"Lord Jesus, You are my rock, my fortress, my strength, and my shield. I put all my trust in You. I repent of only adding You to my life when you deserve to be the center and my everything! I confess and renounce my pride and disobedience; I haven't made Your Word my foundation, nor have I fully obeyed what I've heard or read. Please forgive me. Break up all the faulty foundations of my life. (Name them: pride, fear, lust, deception, etc.) *Establish me in You! Replace my* ___________ (e.g., bitterness) *with Your* ___________ (mercy and grace). *I resist every evil spirit that has had a foothold in my life; I command you to leave me NOW in the powerful name of Jesus Christ! I cancel your assignments against me; I demand that you no longer prey upon my life. I call upon the Lord Jesus as my Deliverer!*

Jesus, please wash me with Your blood. Cleanse the foundation of my life. Heal me of the effects of the traumas and abuse I've endured. Bind up the wounds in my soul; heal my memories and damaged emotions. I forgive everyone who has hurt me. Please forgive me for walking in my iniquity and the iniquity of my ancestors. I receive Your forgiveness; thank You! Consecrate me for Yourself. I will read and study Your Word regularly and apply it to my life. Please teach me, Holy Spirit. Enable me to walk in this new life You have offered me with a firm foundation in You. In Jesus' name, amen."

As the Apostle Paul prayed for the Ephesians, so I pray for you: May the Messiah Jesus *"dwell in your hearts through faith; that you, being rooted* [established and secure] *and grounded* [solidly founded] *in love, may be able to comprehend with all the saints what is the width and length and depth and height—to* know [experientially] *the love of Christ which passes* [head] *knowledge; that you may be filled with all the fullness of God"* (**Eph. 3:17-19**).

"Righteousness and justice are the foundation of Your throne; mercy and truth go before Your face" (**Ps. 89:14**).

TWENTY-NINE

Beliefs Determine Destiny

"And do not be conformed to this world, but be transformed by the renewing of your mind, that you may prove what is that good and acceptable and perfect will of God" (**Rom. 12:2**). *"For as he thinks in his heart, so is he..."* (**Prov. 23:7a**).

Our basic beliefs are those core values that indicate how we perceive our lives. They are fundamental, defining our approach to life. They influence how we respond or react to what happens to us. Most of these beliefs are formed during our childhood, and are based on our experiences and relationships. Those that line up with God's Word are "essential truths," and those that contradict God's truth are "essential lies." Essential truths are beliefs, attitudes, decisions, and expectations that agree with God's Word, Person, and character. Essential lies are beliefs, attitudes, judgments, expectations, and vows that do not agree with God's Word, Person, or character.

Depending on how we are treated at home and socially, we develop beliefs about men, women, parents, other authorities, children, and life in general. These beliefs will directly affect our relationships, choices, and lifestyles. Our societies and cultures contain perceptions and lies that influence our thinking, often without our realizing it. We tend to believe what was taught us as children even when it contradicts what is in the Scriptures.

Our Beliefs Are Critical to Our Lives

Our beliefs about ourselves are the prognosis of what we will become. We are bound by the lies we believe, and we are freed by the truths we believe. We give the enemy the right to trample on us when we believe what he says. If we review the events of our past apart from Jesus' redeeming blood, we can be deceived. We must know what God says about us and line up our beliefs with His. What we believe is critical!

Essential lies are what we believe about ourselves, others, and God that appear to be true (based on the facts of our experience), but are false (based on the truth of God's Word). Though most essential lies are formed during our youth, some are formed later. They are based on hurts we've received, and are usually direct lies told to us by the devil. We believe the lies because they make sense; they fit the painful scenarios we have experienced. Repeated hurts reinforce essential lies.

Essential lies and truths are often passed down through one's family line. We learn our basic central beliefs from our families. These beliefs are rooted in our hearts and reflected in our actions. They are usually embedded deep enough to stay securely fastened even in the face of trauma or stress. Therefore, it is very important that we align our essential beliefs with God's Word. They will directly influence our destiny.

Most of us have at least a few essential lies that dictate expectations and behavior to us. Our behavior often boomerangs off of those lies, setting us up to repeat past negative behavior, which then confirms the lies. If we change our beliefs, our behavior will change. As people of God, we must refuse to embrace lies any longer, and exchange them for the truth of God's Word. We need to know what God says about each situation and agree with Him, choosing *His* truth. *"Sanctify them by Your truth. Your word is truth"* (**John 17:17**).

We need to be renewed in our minds, to see things differently, to change our perspective. The Apostle Paul says to put off the old nature, and *then* put on the new (*see* **Eph. 4:22-23**). We must reject the lies before we can embrace the truth. To believe both at the same time is not possible; one will contradict the other.

Replacing Lies with Truth

1. Identify and write down the lies you believe. To discover the essential lies, examine your life for patterns, hurts, recurring thoughts, or personal issues. Identify your negative emotions (e.g., hurt, anger, resentment, or fear). Ask yourself what lie drives the emotion. What do you believe about God, yourself, or others that is limiting your destiny?

The following lies and opposing truths should help you in identifying your essential lie(s):

- **Lie: *"I am alone."*** This lie inspires fear, which can paralyze us. We fear the unknown; we wonder if God will be with us everywhere, all the time. We feel nervous and indecisive.

  Truth: On the cross, Jesus was alone and forsaken by the Father momentarily so that we would never fear being alone again (*see* **Matt. 27:46, Heb. 13:5**). He *never* leaves us or forsakes us!

- **Lie: *"I do not belong."*** We feel left out, rejected, and separate from others. We lack personal identity.

  Truth: Our acceptance and identity are in Jesus. We are identified and defined by our relationship with Him, not by what the world says about us (*see* **Eph. 1:4-6**).

- **Lie: *"I am not as good as ________."*** We compare ourselves with others. We may feel unloved or loved *less* than someone else, unnoticed, unworthy, and jealous of those who have what we want. We try to prove our worth, but nothing we do seems to be enough to win approval.

  Truth: We are God's workmanship and very precious. The Lord does not compare us with others. He gave each of us gifts and talents and wants us to fulfill our destiny (*see* **Eph. 2:10**).

- **Lie: *"I am not good enough."*** Shame makes us want to cover our failures and imperfections. It says we have crossed a line that is beyond the grace of God. Shame is a blending of guilt and hopelessness and results in self-consciousness and fear.

  Truth: God already knows what we want to hide and loves us anyway. He will forgive us if we confess our sin. God is not separated from us by our failures and needs; nothing can separate us from His love (*see* **Rom. 8:35-39**). Grace is not a salary; it's a gift from God.

- **Lie:** ***"I am not safe."*** We feel insecure, unprotected, and vulnerable. We battle with fear and distrust.

  Truth: We are secure and safe in the Lord, Who is our refuge and deliverer (**Ps. 18:2**). We need not fear when we really know God's love for us (**1 John 4:16, 18**).

- **Lie:** ***"I am ruined for life."*** We feel ashamed, hopeless, disgraced, and defiled. We see ourselves as spoiled goods. A common cause of this is sexual abuse/sin.

  Truth: Your life is not over; God will restore you if you let Him. He can repair whatever damage was done (*see* **Jer. 30:17**).

- **Lie:** ***"I cannot __________."*** You feel defeated and hopeless. This lie may have been triggered by a failure or a major loss.

  Truth: Our hope is in a Person, not in circumstances or in ourselves. We need to look away from our situations and look at Jesus. We are *more* than conquerors through Him Who loved us (**Rom. 8:37**).

2. Replace the lies with truth. The truth should counteract the main issue of the lie. Express it in your own words, not necessarily quoting Scripture, but staying true to it. Make it personal (e.g., *"I am not alone because Jesus said He would never leave me or forsake me. He is always with me."*)

In writing your essential truths, use these questions as a guideline:

- Does it say what God says?
- Does it address the main issue expressed in the essential lie?
- Can you believe it? Does it fit who you really are?

3. Add at least one Scripture that supports the truth. Write it out and try to memorize it so you can quote it to counter the lie if it resurfaces. Write the essential truth with the Scripture on a card that you can keep in your pocket or purse and easily review or refer to when you need it.

4. Pray a prayer of confession. *"Lord, I confess my sin and my ancestors' sin of believing the lie that ___________. I forgive those who hurt me and were a factor in my forming this lie* (name the people). *Please forgive me, Father, for believing this and for allowing it to dictate behavior to me. Forgive me for judging myself and others based on it. I know the blood of Jesus is sufficient for this sin, so I receive Your forgiveness gratefully. I renounce and break my agreement with this lie, with the kingdom of darkness, and with the enemy. I choose to accept and believe the truth that _____________. Please cement your truth in my heart and mind. May I be renewed by it, restored to the original glory You gave me, and set apart to do all Your will. In Jesus' name, amen."*

5. Meditate on the essential truth for a month, quoting it daily. Establishing a new thinking pattern takes time. Make sure the truth becomes permanent in your mind. The enemy will likely challenge it; he loves to repeat old lies to us to get us to believe them again so that he can enslave us. *"The thief does not come except to steal, and to kill, and to destroy. I have come that they may have life, and that they may have it more abundantly"* (**John 10:10**). *"The thoughts of the righteous are right..."* (**Prov. 12:5a**).

"For though we walk in the flesh, we do not war according to the flesh. For the weapons of our warfare are not carnal but mighty in God for pulling down strongholds, casting down arguments and every high thing that exalts itself against the knowledge of God, bringing every thought into captivity to the obedience of Christ" (**2 Cor. 10:3-5**).

THIRTY

Curses and Their Causes

"Christ has redeemed us from the curse of the law, having become a curse for us (for it is written, 'Cursed is everyone who hangs on a tree'), that the blessing of Abraham might come upon the Gentiles in Christ Jesus, that we might receive the promise of the Spirit through faith" (**Gal. 3:13-14**).

If you do not sense God's blessing and favor in your life, you could be living under a curse. Although Jesus redeemed us from the curse of the law (the guilt and penalty of having broken His law), we can still be susceptible to curses if we have not cancelled family/ancestral curses and confessed family iniquity, or if we have been disobedient to the Scriptures (thereby bringing a curse upon ourselves). Until we deal specifically with these open doors, the devil has a legal right to harass us. Removing his right to curse us through confession, repentance, forgiveness, and obedience gives us authority to cancel the curses.

Common Curses and Their Causes

1. The curse of poverty (**Deut. 28:29-30**) can be seen when business ventures frequently fail, when one struggles financially although his income appears to be sufficient (the money seems to be devoured), homes or cars are repossessed, and family members cannot manage or save money, or be thrifty. The curse of poverty can be over a country or a nationality. (Don't assume a curse is present hastily; some people are disorganized, lazy, and undisciplined in saving and spending.)

Causes: robbery, fraud, witchcraft, trusting in man rather than in God, robbing God of tithes and offerings (**Mal. 3:8-9**), swearing falsely in God's name (**Zech. 5:4**); anti-Semitism (**Gen. 12:1-3**), refusing to give to the poor (**Prov. 27:27**), and oppression of and injustice toward the weak and helpless (**Prov. 22:22-23**).

2. The curse of robbery might be behind fraud, a loss of houses or properties, a frozen inheritance, or frequent theft.

Causes: robbery, fraud, illegal traffic of merchandise, a slave trade, or human trafficking (**Zech. 5:3-4**).

3. The curse of female problems is revealed when within a family there are numerous miscarriages, still births, unusually difficult deliveries, or extremely painful or abnormal menstrual cycles.

Causes: Incest, adultery, divorce, sexual perversion, pornography, abortion, fornication, sexual abuse, and rebellion (**Gen. 3:16, Lev. 18**).

4. The curse of strange, untimely deaths or multiple family suicides can indicate a curse. In Ralph's family, each man had a heart attack and died by the age of 45. Ralph broke the curse of death, resisted a spirit of infirmity, and lived to be an elderly gentleman. In another family, there were seven suicides in the same generation, indicating a curse.

Causes: homicide, shedding blood, idolatry, witchcraft, and love of money (**Prov. 2:22; Ps. 37:28**).

5. The curse of recurring illnesses in the family bloodline (spirits of infirmity) may result in blood diseases, cancers, heart disease, and arthritis. A believing family of seven adult children approached a pastor for help because they all were experiencing serious illnesses and financial ruin. Through researching the family history, the pastor discovered that their mother had cursed each of them. Once the curses were broken, the situations were prayed for, and healing and financial blessing followed.

Causes: witchcraft (**2 Chron. 33:6, 2 Cor. 6:14-15, 17**), curses placed on a person or family (**Deut. 28:27, 35**), shedding blood, idolatry, and pledges or oaths to ungodly associations.

6. The curse of being accident-prone is seen when one is unusually clumsy, and/or bad things happen to him frequently.

Causes: homicide, spiritualism, witchcraft and idolatry (**Deut. 5:7-9**).

7. The curse of unusual family discord is revealed by excessive strife and a lack of favor and unity between family members (even though they may be believers).

Causes: abuse, slander, gossip (**Ps. 53:4**); disrespect for parents (**Eph. 6:1-3, Prov. 20:20**).

8. The curse of demonic oppression is revealed by psychic abilities, mental or emotional bondages, compulsive behaviors, or extreme spiritual or emotional heaviness.

Causes: witchcraft, curses placed by someone involved in witchcraft, ancestors involved in the occult, and words or prayers that control, manipulate, or hurt.

9. The curse of mental illness or insanity is revealed by debilitating fears, psychoses, bipolar disorder, confusion, indecisiveness, and dementia.

Causes: pride, haughtiness, trust in riches, and stubbornness (**Dan. 4:28-32, Deut. 28:28**).

10. The curse of homelessness may rest on vagabonds, those exiled from their countries, or those who are living illegally in foreign nations.

Causes: homicide, trusting in riches (**Gen. 4:12, Ps. 109:10**), sexual sin, and disobedience to God.

Generational Curses

"You shall not make for yourself a carved image...you shall not bow down to them nor serve them. For I, the Lord your God, am a jealous God, visiting the iniquity of the fathers upon the children to the third and fourth generations of those who hate Me, but showing mercy to thousands, to those who love Me and keep My commandments" (**Ex. 20:4-6**). *"Our fathers have sinned and are not, and we have borne their iniquities"* (**Lam. 5:7**).

The iniquity of one's forefathers is passed down to the third and fourth generations, affecting their descendants unless it is confessed and the pattern broken in Jesus' name. Four generations add up to 32 forefathers, so we can "inherit" numerous sin issues, character defects, and illnesses that our parents and those before them had if they were not victorious over them.

Generational curses get worse with each generation. However, God's mercy follows those who are obedient and extends to thousands of generations. How important it is to live victoriously in obedience! It is the best inheritance we can offer our descendants.

To Break a Curse

1. Try to determine the cause of the curse. Examine your life and that of your ancestors.

2. Repent of and renounce the iniquity and disobedience linked to the cause. Uproot it from your spirit and soul by declaring that Jesus' blood is sufficient for all iniquity. Renounce Satan and all of his works in Jesus' mighty name.

3. Revoke and cancel the curses in Jesus' name, including racial and national curses. Break their power from your life.

4. Claim the victory that is yours in Jesus because of His crucifixion and resurrection. *"...if the Son makes you free, you shall be free indeed"* (**John 8:36**).

5. Thank God for breaking the curses, and ask for His blessings to replace them. Proclaim God's Word over your life, which will release His blessing further.

"And all these blessings shall come upon you and overtake you, because you obey the voice of the Lord your God: blessed shall you be in the city, and blessed shall you be in the country... Blessed shall you be when you come in, and blessed shall you be when you go out. The Lord will cause your enemies who rise against you to be defeated before your face... The Lord will command the blessing on you in your storehouses and in all to which you set your hand, and He will bless you in the land which the Lord your God is giving you" (**Deut. 28:2-3, 6-8**).

THIRTY-ONE

Reverse the Curse!

"Now Jabez was more honorable than his brothers, and his mother called his name Jabez, saying, 'Because I bore him in pain.' And Jabez called on the God of Israel saying, 'Oh, that You would bless me indeed, and enlarge my territory, that Your hand would be with me, and that You would keep me from evil, that I may not cause pain!' So, God granted him what he requested" (**1 Chron. 4:9-10**).

Although all mothers experience pain when giving birth, Jabez's mother must have endured more pain than usual. At his circumcision, she wanted it to be known that *he* was the one who had caused her such misery! So she named him Jabez, which means, *"He will cause pain."* Not only did she make public his initial infliction of pain upon her, she also put a word curse on him that he would *always* be a source of pain! Every time Jabez heard his name, he was reminded of the grief he had caused. Perhaps he believed that he would never bring joy or pleasure to anyone. There was no hope for him *except* to hurt others, for that was the curse over his life. Jabez lived according to his name; he caused pain.

But one day, he had had enough! He called on the name of the God of Israel, begging Him to intervene in his life and destiny. He pleaded with Him for blessing. He asked God to lift his ceiling of failure and limitation, and to extend his borders. He asked for God's hand of protection to be upon him. Jabez cried out to God to free him from the word curse that had destined him for failure. He was tired of the years of pain and problems; he knew only God could turn his life around. And God granted his request!

Jewish writers affirm that Jabez became an eminent doctor in the law whose reputation drew so many disciples and scribes around him that a town was named after him as noted in **1 Chron. 2:55**. His testimony, *"Jabez was more honorable than his brothers"* (**1 Chron. 4:9**), spoke of his virtue, vocational success, victory in warfare, and respect for his mother and others.

God obviously answered his prayer and turned his life from one of failure and pain to one of success and blessing. What God did for Jabez, He can and wants to do for you! He can cancel the curses that have been placed on you and bring you into a broad place of blessing. He can lift every ceiling on your development and break every curse of failure. If you will cry out to the God of Israel to rescue you, He will hear and save you.

Let's pray this prayer of Jabez before we look at specific word curses to break. *"God of Israel, I cry out to you today! Oh, that in blessing, You would bless me indeed! Cancel any limits placed on me so that I can be who You created me to be and do what You have called me to do. Break the power of failure from my life. Enlarge and expand my territory and borders. Let Your hand of protection, guidance, and blessing be upon me. Keep me from evil; help me to always choose Your paths of righteousness so that I will not cause pain to anyone."*

Curses can come upon us as a result of personal disobedience, negative words spoken directly to, about, or over us, or curses from witches. We can also invite curses by the negative things we say about ourselves. The late author and Bible teacher, Derek Prince, wrote *"The main vehicle for both blessing and cursing is words... spoken, written, or uttered inwardly."*

Names can be prophetic declarations that define our identity. We perform according to what we believe about ourselves. Words spoken to us become names and descriptions that we carry in our hearts; they determine our actions. Great names can release power into our lives and bring us into our God-given destinies. A prophetic declaration releases grace to accomplish what it says. In the same way, damaging words curse us and limit our future.

Common Causes of Word Curses

1. binding words spoken by people with relational authority — Words spoken by people in authority have great power over our lives — more so than those by people with whom we have little relationship.

When parents tell their children that they are good for nothing, those words can cause the children to make mistakes, be accident-prone and careless, or fail at work or in relationships. When parents or teachers say in exasperation to a child, *"You'll never learn,"* the child may develop learning problems as a result of that curse. If a church leader says to a congregant, *"God will never use you,"* those words can bind that person to uselessness in the kingdom of God. If a husband tells his wife *"You are a terrible homemaker,"* no matter how hard she tries, she will not be able to keep the house clean and organized. Her husband's words will put a ceiling on her abilities.

"Death and life are in the power of the tongue, and those who love it will eat its fruit" (**Prov. 18:21**). Words give the enemy a foothold for attack just as they give the Lord an opportunity to bless. Words set in motion what will lead to life and health or to death and destruction.

2. self-imposed word curses — When we speak negatively about ourselves, we give the enemy an opportunity to attack us. Our words directly affect our lives. *"A fool's mouth is his destruction, and his lips are the snare of his soul"* (**Prov. 18:7**). *"You are snared by the words of your mouth; you are taken by the words of your mouth"* (**Prov. 6:2**).

Examples of self-imposed curses are:

- *"I'm accident-prone."*
- *"I get the flu every year."*
- *"I'm dead tired!"*

Be careful how you speak and what you say. Your words become the framework by which your life is built. **Hebrews 11:3b** says, *"...the worlds were framed by the word of God, so that the things which are seen were not made of things which are visible."* Since we are made in His image, our words are creative. Our worlds (lives) are framed by our words.

3. childhood promises — When we are hurt as children, we tend to make promises to ourselves to get revenge and to avoid more pain.

These promises or inner vows are directives sent through the heart and mind to the body. Even when they have been forgotten by the conscious mind, the programming of those promises is still intact and functioning. We do not grow out of inner vows, but we can break them in the name of Jesus.

Examples of promises children make to themselves:

- *"I will never be like Mom! She is always late and embarrasses me."*
- *"I'll never let anyone get close enough to hurt me again."*
- *"I won't try anything new so that I won't fail."*

4. damaging words spoken by others — Although hurtful words are most powerful when spoken by relational authorities, *any* destructive word can bind us. Every spoken word releases life or death; even words said by people we don't know can impact us. Slander, gossip, and criticism can result in bondage. When children or teenagers speak in anger to one another, the mean things they say can cause torment for years. Try to feel the anguish of those who might hear sentences like these:

- *"You're a reject! You're stupid!"*
- *"You're fat. You're lazy and good for nothing."*
- *"We don't want you to be on our team. You don't play well."*

5. prayers to control, accuse, or hurt — When we pray for others, we must pray in line with God's Word and will. Prayers that originate from selfish desires or wrong motives can be detrimental to those for whom we pray. If our prayers are contrary to God's will for their lives, confusion can result. Carnal, manipulative prayers can cause bondage and demonic attack.

Claiming a certain person to be your spouse can prevent that one from marrying the right person. Claiming a particular piece of property can bind that property from going into the right hands and being used for God's purposes. Ask the Lord to inspire your prayers!

Finding Freedom from Word Curses

1. Forgive everyone who has spoken against you. Bless them in Jesus' name. *"...bless those who curse you..."* (**Matt. 5:44**). Make a conscious decision not to receive the curse or negative words. Guard what you believe.

"Lord, I forgive _____ for speaking against me. I reject those negative words, and refuse to believe them or let them dictate to me. I cancel their effects in Jesus' name! I bless _______, and ask You to bless them, too."

2. Break the power of every word curse spoken against you in Jesus' name.

"I break the power of every word curse spoken to or over me in the mighty name of Jesus! I specifically break the power of these words: _____________. (Name any word curse(s) you've received.) *I nullify every binding word over my life, and I receive the inheritance and blessings that come from above. Thank You, Lord."*

3. Ask God to heal the wounds that are attached to the hurtful names you have been called. Jabez was so named because of the pain he caused at birth, so the wound to be prayed into for him would be the pain his mother experienced in delivery.

"Lord, please heal my soul from the wounds associated with the hurtful names I've been called. I especially pray for all the wound(s) of ____________. Please heal my corresponding damaged emotions."

4. Ask God to break the power of slander and gossip against you. Nullify their effects in Jesus' name. Forgive and bless your accusers.

"Father, please heal my heart and emotions from criticism, gossip, and slander. Break the power of those words from me; nullify their effects. I will not be or do what they accuse me of, in Jesus' name! That's not me! I forgive and bless them. If there is any *truth to what they say, please reveal it to me so that I might make things right."*

5. Repent of and renounce all childhood promises and declarations that are contrary to God's Word. Repent of all desire for revenge and self-preservation. Ask the Lord to forgive you and release you from the promises you made to yourself.

"I repent of and renounce the declarations I made as a child that are contrary to Your Word. I confess as sin my promise that I would get even with _______. Today I forgive them for _________. Please forgive me for my bitterness and desire for revenge. Release me from this promise and all promises that I made to myself in ignorance and bitterness. I choose to be led by Your Spirit, not driven by childhood oaths. Thank You, Father."

6. Declare the truth of God's Word against every lie you have heard or believed. Claim His words of life to overcome the negative words of failure and death. *"Your Word has given me life"* **(Ps. 119:50b)**. Quote the Scriptures over yourself every day.

"In the authority of Jesus my Messiah, I cut myself free from _______'s words that ____________ (e.g., I am a failure), and I smash those words as lies from the enemy. I break their power over me in Jesus' name! 'I can do all things through Christ Who strengthens me!' Lord, I embrace Your truth and I believe it rather than what I have been told. Please set me free according to Your Word! In Jesus' name, amen."

Psalm 119:50 says, *"This is my comfort in my affliction, for Your word has given me life."* God's Word creates and releases life. Read it, sing it, claim it, pray it, and believe it! Speak life, victory, and blessing over people. If you're in authority over others, encourage and affirm them. Appreciate their efforts. Affirm your spouse, children, and friends. Try to express appreciation and affirmation as much as possible to as many people as possible every day!

THIRTY-TWO

Freedom from the Curse of Barrenness

" 'Sing, O barren, you who have not borne! Break forth into singing, and cry aloud, you who have not labored with child! For more are the children of the desolate than the children of the married woman,' says the Lord. Enlarge the place of your tent, and let them stretch out the curtains of your dwellings; do not spare; lengthen your cords, and strengthen your stakes. For you shall expand to the right and to the left, and your descendants will inherit the nations, and make the desolate cities inhabited" (**Isa. 54:1-3**).

Children were a very important part of the economic structure of the ancient Middle East. They were a source of labor for the family and were responsible to care for their elderly parents. So, barrenness was considered a curse. A childless wife felt tremendous disappointment and humiliation. She was acutely aware that she would not be able to give her husband a son to carry on his family name. A barren wife was often obligated by custom to give one of the servant girls to her husband to bear children for her. A man was even legally permitted to divorce a barren wife.

Barrenness is not limited to a physical condition, though. It can extend into many areas of life. We can be barren of loving relationships, finances, and our determined destiny. We can be barren of hope, joy, and passion. We can have no interest in or desire for our spouse. Our souls may resemble a desert: dry, dusty, and lifeless. Having no anticipation of better days, we may be hurt and angry that our lives have turned out as they have. Disappointment and anger feed the barrenness as we despise the direction our lives have gone. There is an emptiness and ache deep within that we cannot shake off. We don't walk tall and with purpose; our souls are bowed down.

Barrenness does not only indicate a lack of life, it can also rob us of what life we *do* have. When we are barren, our words don't overflow with God's power, grace, and healing; they are lifeless and contain elements of weariness, discouragement, and/or bitterness.

Barrenness can result from neglecting the secret place of prayer. If we do not have intimate times with our Bridegroom, Jesus, we will have no life, no offspring, no fruit. We have little passion for pursuing Him and His will. We will receive no new vision or fresh revelation. We just have a dry, casual relationship with the Lord. We need to return to Jesus with all of our hearts, and repent for our wandering and neglect. We may need to fast from food and entertainment in order to press into Him. If we seek Him diligently, we will find Him!

Barrenness that Leads to Life

There is a form of barrenness that actually leads to life. In ancient times, when God needed a person to fulfill a particular vacancy or to meet a specific need (e.g., a prophet or forerunner), He inspired a barren woman to desperately seek Him in prayer, pleading for a child. When God opened her womb in response to prayer, He put into motion His purposes for which the child to be born was a key player. When God broke the curse of barrenness over the lives of the following women, each one gave birth to a man chosen by God to have a significant ministry. When the curse of barrenness was broken, a life marked by God followed. (And when barrenness is broken off of us, we, too, will see our lives marked by God!)

Rachel, Jacob's wife, was barren for years until she gave birth to Joseph. **Genesis 30:22** says, *"God remembered Rachel and God listened to her..."* Joseph was sold into slavery as a teenager, but later rose to power and saved multitudes from starvation. He was God's chosen man to save the Hebrews at that time.

Hannah was barren until God heard her cries and granted her a son, whom she named Samuel. Samuel became a significant prophet of God (*see* **1 Sam. 3:19-20**). He anointed the first two kings over Israel and was considered Israel's main prophet for decades. He not only functioned in that gift himself; he also birthed schools of prophets.

Elizabeth was barren until she was too old to bear children (*see* **Luke 1:5-7**). The angel Gabriel prophesied to Zacharias (her old husband) that she would give birth. Zacharias questioned the possibility of that due to their old age (v.18), but Elizabeth did conceive and miraculously gave birth to John (v. 25).

A portion of Zecharias' prophecy over his son is found in **Luke 1:76-79**, *"And you, child, will be called the prophet of the Highest; for you will go before the face of the Lord to prepare His ways, to give knowledge of salvation to His people by the remission of their sins, through the tender mercy of our God, with which the Dayspring from on high has visited us; to give light to those who sit in darkness and the shadow of death, to guide our feet into the way of peace."* John was the forerunner of the Messiah. He called Israel back to God through repentance and water baptism, and cleared the way for Jesus to begin His earthly ministry.

If you are feeling barren and dry in your walk with God, discipline yourself to seek Him more earnestly. God may want to do spiritually with you what He did naturally with these women. He may want to plant something in your spirit that will bear His image and fulfill His purposes. What He impregnates you with will grow and take form as you pray. You may feel moody, be easily irritated and frustrated with your circumstances, experience pressure within, and feel restless in your spirit. All of this is to force you to press into God and to pray more frequently and intensely.

After a season of carrying this new life in prayer, you will "travail" it into being. This is God's offspring, but He needs you to conceive it in intimacy with Him. You are to pray as it takes shape during the spiritual gestation period, and give birth to it in His timing and His way. Don't rely on your own understanding or fall prey to pride or fear. This is something of God, and you are the humble, willing vessel to birth it. The new thing could be a book you write, a worship CD you produce, a ministry you start, or a shift in what you now do or where you serve. Spiritual pregnancy may lead to *major* transition in your life!

Barrenness that Leads to Death

There is another form of barrenness—one that is destructive. It's a curse that gains a foothold due to personal sin and/or iniquity (see Chapter 17). God wants us to bear new life, so we must find the cause of the barrenness, confess it, and return to serving the Lord with joy.

A common cause of such barrenness is to despise an authority figure. 2 Samuel 6:20-23 speaks of Michal who despised her husband, King David, in her heart. From then on, she was barren. This could mean that David never again had intimate relations with her or that she never could conceive again. When a woman despises her husband, it creates barrenness in her relationship with him. She resents and judges him, and rejects his overtures of love. The tenderness she once felt for him is replaced by resentment. She merely puts up with him—or worse, speaks evil to him or about him. Before long, she will find that her marriage does not bear good fruit or satisfy her. She loses her desire for her husband; he may sense or feel that and withdraw from her. Then the cycle of barrenness worsens.

Some people experience barrenness because they despise their parents. By rejecting the counsel and wisdom of one's parents, a person can set himself up for making major mistakes (*see* **Prov. 23:22, 25**). Despising teachers or coaches can result in low performance. Despising pastors or Bible teachers can prevent spiritual development and understanding.

When we ignore or neglect the spiritual gifts God has given us, we are guilty of despising them. We will be held accountable before God for how we used His gifts. Speaking evil of political leaders can open the door to the enemy in *our* lives and result in a loss of freedom or peace in a city or nation. We need to pray for governmental leaders, not judge or slander them.

Freedom from Sin-induced Barrenness

1. To secure freedom from the curse of barrenness, make a list of the people, ethnic groups, or positions that you despise. Confess this grievous sin to the Lord and ask for His forgiveness and cleansing.

2. Repent of having a hard heart and resenting authorities and leaders. Renounce your judgments of them and the pride and anger that are associated with your attitudes of judgment.

3. Forgive those who have disappointed, offended, and betrayed you. Forgive your parents, spouse, and children. Release them and your hurt to the Lord. Forgive anyone else whom you resent.

4. Ask the Lord to restore you to a place of fruitfulness. Sing over the barrenness of your soul (**Isa. 54:1**). Worship the Lord! Let His presence and love fill and heal your heart. When God heals barrenness, He heals amazingly! God doesn't just care for the poor, needy, and barren; He also grants them a home and lifts them into a place of royalty.

"He raises the poor out of the dust, and lifts the needy out of the ash heap, that He may seat him with princes—with the princes of His people. He grants the barren woman a home, like a joyful mother of children. Praise the Lord!" (**Ps. 113:7-9**)

THIRTY-THREE

The Bondage of Shame

"Now early in the morning He came again into the temple, and all the people came to Him; and He sat down and taught them. Then the scribes and Pharisees brought to Him a woman caught in adultery. And when they had set her in the midst, they said to Him, 'Teacher, this woman was caught in adultery, in the very act. Now Moses, in the law, commanded us that such should be stoned. But what do You say?' This they said, testing Him, that they might have something of which to accuse Him. But Jesus stooped down and wrote on the ground with His finger, as though He did not hear. So when they continued asking Him, He raised Himself up and said to them, 'He who is without sin among you, let him throw a stone at her first.' And again He stooped down and wrote on the ground. Then those who heard it, being convicted by their conscience, went out one by one, beginning with the oldest even to the last. And Jesus was left alone, and the woman standing in the midst. When Jesus had raised Himself up and saw no one but the woman, He said to her, 'Woman, where are those accusers of yours? Has no one condemned you?' She said, 'No one, Lord.' And Jesus said to her, 'Neither do I condemn you; go and sin no more'" (**John 8:2-11**).

In Greek, verse three literally says, *"a woman taken with shame upon her."* To stand before this group of condemning, religious men added to the shame she already felt from her sin and exposure. She was humiliated, publicly criticized, and treated as an object of contempt.

Shame is one of the most common reasons people live defeated and powerless lives. Widespread in the Body of Messiah, it causes a person to question God's love, acceptance, and forgiveness. Shame leaves a stain on the fabric of the soul. It is a barrier to close friendships and to success in business. Because it is debilitating, it is a favorite tool of the enemy to wield. Look at the following characteristics to see if shame has a prominent place in your life.

Basic Characteristics of Shame

1. negative self-image — No matter how many good things are happening in your life, little of it matters to you because of how you feel about yourself. You battle with self-pity and self-reproach. You may take on self-destructive behaviors such as anorexia or bulimia, cutting, or other forms of self-abuse.

2. performance conscious — You measure your worth by what you produce or accomplish, as if it will give you value in the eyes of others. Your performance may become addictive, showing up in over-commitment to work or ministry. You always feel you are "on."

3. people pleaser — You are anxious to please and be needed. You make it your job to ensure that everything is running smoothly and everyone is happy. You find it almost impossible to say no to requests.

4. tired, apathetic, lacking in creativity — You fear failure, so, you refuse to take risks. You are weighed down by life. Burdens overwhelm you, and you seldom feel joy.

5. lack personal boundaries — You're not sure where you "end" and others "begin." You reveal inappropriate personal details of your life to people whom you barely know in an attempt to feel connected to someone. You allow others to make decisions for you because you feel your opinion isn't worth much.

6. ignore personal needs — Because shame tells you that you are no good, you tend to ignore your legitimate needs. You feel it is more important to please others than to care for yourself.

7. cannot bear criticism — When someone says, "You made a mistake," you hear, "You *are* a mistake." You hear criticism as rejection, so criticism devastates you.

8. afraid to confront — Because you have little confidence in yourself, you are easily intimidated. You bear and bury offense instead of confronting the offender.

9. find it difficult to trust — You are on guard when around people, wondering what their agenda is for your life. It is hard for you to let anyone in, because you're sure they will not like what they see. This behavior can border on paranoia. You develop facades and masks and distance yourself from others, fearing their rejection. You sub-consciously think, "*How can anyone like me when I don't like myself?*"

10. possessive in relationships — Due to feelings of unworthiness and a fear of abandonment, you cling to the people in your life, afraid that if they leave, no one will take their place. You are emotionally dependent on them.

11. controlling — Life is frightening to you; the only bearable way to survive is to maintain control. If you don't control the circumstances around you, people might find out what caused your shame.

In the sub-surface of your life, are there hidden issues that have never been dealt with (e.g., a broken heart, grief, loss, hopelessness, rebellion, or resentment) and inner wounds that have never healed? If you nurse them, shame will become your identity. Shame festers in the wounded.

What Causes Shame?

Shame is usually caused by a strong sense of guilt, embarrassment, unworthiness, or disgrace. Rejection is at its root. Anything that sets you apart from others makes you vulnerable to shame: your weight, height, nationality, complexion, or birthmarks. Any place where you compare yourself with others and feel you don't quite measure up can lead to shame.

Shame is also caused by personal sin (one devastating moment or a lifestyle) or by another's sin against us, such as abandonment, abuse, or betrayal. Rejection by those we love makes us feel ashamed.

Shame can be caused by hurtful words such as put-downs, nicknames, or statements like: *"You're so stupid!"* Even words said in fun can be hurtful. They can make us feel we're not worthy of love or trust.

Sometimes we feel shame over our needs for affirmation, affection, and acceptance. When these needs are not met, we feel rejected and are ashamed that no one cares for us. Abused children often feel ashamed of the abuse they have suffered. Somehow they feel responsible.

A lack of parental blessing is a common cause of shame. A parental blessing consists of affection, discipline, a projected future, quality time, and a close relationship between parent and child. When parents fail to bless their children, shame fills the vacuum.

What the Bible Says about Shame

"Do not fear, for you will not be ashamed; neither be disgraced, for you will not be put to shame; for you will forget the shame of your youth, and will not remember the reproach of your widowhood anymore" **(Isa. 54:4)**. *"You shall eat in plenty and be satisfied, and praise the name of the Lord your God, Who has dealt wondrously with you; and My people shall never be put to shame"* **(Joel 2:26)**. *"As it is written: 'Behold, I lay in Zion a stumbling stone and rock of offense, and whoever believes on Him will not be put to shame'"* **(Rom. 9:33)**.

The Scriptures are clear that shame is not God's intention for His people. In the story of the adulterous woman, Jesus bent down to write on the ground. His writing took attention off of the woman and onto what He was doing. Jesus was covering and protecting her, just as He does with us. He doesn't deal with our sin as the Pharisees did with hers.

Jesus saw that they were after *rightness* not *righteousness*. He put an end to their questioning by saying, *"You who are without sin, throw the first stone."* Jesus did not shame them; He just reminded them that they too, were not innocent. Then He stooped again to write on the ground. He didn't want to embarrass the woman; He covered her nakedness and shame. Jesus then spoke directly to her with respect. She stood *guilty*, but not *condemned* by Jesus. He used the respectful title "woman" with her—the same title He used with His mother.

Jesus pardoned her as He does us! He hasn't changed. Still today, He wants to cover and restore, not expose and shame.

Countering Shame's Lies

Shame says, *"You're dirty, defiled, tarnished."* But Jesus washes us with His blood, which cleanses us from ALL sin.

Shame says, *"Hide; don't tell anyone your secret sin and failure!"* But **James 5:16a** says, *"Confess your trespasses to one another, and pray for one another, that you may be healed..."* Find someone you can share openly with. Admit past hurt, abuse, failures, or sin. Refuse to live in denial anymore. St. Augustine said, *"If we want to be free, we must first undeceive ourselves."*

At some point, you need to take the protective coverings off of your wounds and failures and let them heal. They need exposure to light. When you share your secret with a trusted friend and are loved in spite of it, you realize you don't have to be ashamed anymore. Talking about it is healing.

Shame says, *"You're worthless. You have no value."* Yet God loves you in spite of your sin and shame. He says, *"Run to Me. I'll cover you."*

His Word says, *"But now, thus says the Lord, who created you, O Jacob, and He who formed you, O Israel: 'Fear not, for I have redeemed you; I have called you by your name; you are Mine... Since you are precious in My sight, you have been honored, and I have loved you...'"* (**Isa. 43:1, 4**).

God's unconditional love for you gives you value! He chose you to be His. You cannot earn His love. Your value is set at what it cost Him to purchase you—the blood of His own Son. You have worth because God declared it so at the cross!

Shame says, *"You can't and you never will. You are a failure!"* You are free from the curse of failure because Jesus became a curse for you on the cross. He broke the curse of failure!

God's Word says, *"I can do all things through Christ Who strengthens me"* (**Phil. 4:13**).

"Most assuredly, I say to you, he who believes in Me, the works that I do he will do also; and greater works than these he will do, because I go to My Father" (**John 14:12**).

Shame says, *"You'll never amount to anything. There is no recovery for you."* God says, *"For I will restore health to you and heal you of your wounds..."* (**Jer. 30:17**). God wants to free you from what has bound you in the past. He wants to restore you and give you *"a future and a hope"* (**Jer. 29:11**).

Accepting God's Forgiveness

You may say, *"God could never forgive what I've done"* or *"God may forgive me, but He'll never feel the same about me again."* The wounds you bear and the shame of your past have kept you in chains. Emotionally, you're bent over; you live with depression or anger, inferiority, and self-pity. Perhaps you have done things that have changed your perception of who you are, like the lost son in **Luke 15:21**, where he said, *"Father, I have sinned against heaven and in your sight, and am no longer worthy to be called your son."* But in Luke 15:22-24, we see the father's readiness to forgive and restore his son the moment he came back. His love knew no limits, his forgiveness no boundaries, his joy no restraint when he welcomed his lost son home. This is what our God is like!

Jesus, the sinless Son of God Who took the sins of the whole world upon Himself, showed us God's extravagant love on the cross. God's love far outweighs the pain in our inner man; knowing and receiving His love and forgiveness frees us from the debilitating shame of our past. Because our sins and failures are under the blood of Jesus, we can have a testimony like this: *"I have done horrible things in my past. I can bring up memories, but it's only past tense. It's not present today. I've been cleansed. My past doesn't affect how I see God, myself, or others. God isn't shaming me; He's forgiven me. There is no record of my sin in heaven."*

Jesus is not ashamed of us. We are part of His family. We belong! God our Father wants us to be so grounded in His love that we are secure in Him and totally free from shame and its expressions in our lives (*see* **Rom. 8:31-39**).

"For both He Who sanctifies [making men holy] and those who are sanctified all have one [Father]. For this reason He is not ashamed to call them brethren" **(Heb. 2:11**, Amplified Bible**)**.

פאר תחת אפר

THIRTY-FOUR

From Shame to Glory

"Neither fornicators, nor idolaters, nor adulterers, nor homosexuals, nor sodomites, nor thieves, nor covetous, nor drunkards, nor revilers, nor extortioners will inherit the kingdom of God. And such were some of you. But you were washed, but you were sanctified, but you were justified in the name of the Lord Jesus and by the Spirit of our God" (**1 Cor. 6:9b-11**). *"I sought the Lord, and He heard me, and delivered me from all my fears. They looked to Him and were radiant, and their faces were not ashamed"* (**Ps. 34:4-5**). *"And the glory which You gave Me I have given them..."* (**John 17:22**).

Glory is God's intention for all creation. The Bible speaks of the glory of nature, man, kings, nations, and Heaven. Most often the word "glory" is used in reference to God Himself. Man's glory comes from being made in God's image. *"Then God said, 'Let Us make man in Our image, according to Our likeness...' So God created man in His own image; in the image of God He created him; male and female He created them"* (**Gen. 1:26-27**).

Glory is God's gift to us. It's our birthright, our God-given DNA. But when sin entered the Garden of Eden, the glory that Adam and Eve had was marred. They exited the garden bent over with shame. When we allow shame to redefine us, we, like Esau, are guilty of selling our birthright (**Gen. 25:29-34**). We are despising our God-given inheritance of glory. We need to be like Jacob, who valued the birthright and the promises of God and was determined to receive them. We need to receive and guard our glory from God and not let anything cloud, mar, or steal it. *"Moreover whom He predestined, these He also called; whom He called, these He also justified and whom He justified these He also glorified"* (**Rom. 8:30**).

Steps toward Freedom from Shame

1. Ask the Holy Spirit to show you the causes of any shame you bear. Is it personal sin or the sin of another against you? Hurtful words to or about you? Unmet needs? A lack of parental blessing?

2. Confess, repent, and forgive, as the Spirit leads you. Read back over the basic characteristics of shame in Chapter 33. Confess any sin you are guilty of and repent of any behaviors you have developed as a reaction to being shamed. Forgive others for their sins against you.

3. Ask God to remove all shame from your soul and to uproot it from the fabric of your life. Break the power of the hurtful words and their effects on you. Ask the Lord to heal your emotions and to cleanse the memories that are connected with shame. Ask Him to meet your needs for love and affirmation and give you His Parental blessing. Ask God to help you form new behavioral patterns. Consider getting an accountability partner to help you be faithful to the lifestyle choices you are making.

4. Read and believe the Scriptures and line up your life with them. It took years for you to develop the shame patterns that you have been walking in, and it could take some time for you to learn to walk free of them. Don't give up!

5. Cultivate intimacy with God the Father. Listen for His voice daily; spend time enjoying His presence. He is *Adonai Rophecha* (Hebrew)—the Lord Who heals you (*see* **Ex. 15:26**).

Suggested Prayer

"Father, thank You for choosing me and conferring Your holiness upon me. Thank you for welcoming me into Your family. Please set me free from the stronghold of shame. I forgive those who have shamed me: __________ (name them). *Forgive me for turning the glory You have given me into shame by walking in shame in these ways:* ___________ (look at the list in the previous chapter).

"Forgive me for not believing what You say about me. I apologize for selling my birthright. I renounce shame and refuse to live under it any longer. I break its power over me by the blood of Jesus, and I reject it, with all of its debilitating effects, in Jesus' name! I will not walk bent over but will stand tall and confident in who You say I am: washed, sanctified, justified, chosen, and beloved. I am Your child, seated in heavenly places with You (*see* **Eph. 2:6**).

"I receive ***Psalm 21:5-7*** *for myself: 'My glory is great in Your salvation; honor and majesty You have placed upon me. For You have made me most blessed forever; You have made me exceedingly glad with Your presence. For I trust in the Lord and through the mercy of the Most High I shall not be moved.' Amen!"*

"What is man that You are mindful of him, and the son of man that You visit him? For You have made him a little lower than the angels, and You have crowned him with glory and honor" (**Ps. 8:4-5**). *"For the Lord God is a sun and shield; the Lord will give grace and glory; no good thing will He withhold from those who walk uprightly. O Lord of hosts, blessed is the man who trusts in You"* (**Ps. 84:11-12**).

THIRTY-FIVE

The Power of the Cross

"For the message of the cross is foolishness to those who are perishing, but to us who are being saved it is the power of God" **(1 Cor. 1:18)**.

I've chosen to put this chapter last as it ties everything together. It's at the cross where we receive all that Jesus died to provide for us. If we preach salvation without preaching the cross, dying to self, and living a surrendered life to the Lord, then we are preaching a flawed gospel. And if we preach the cross without emphasizing the importance of a personal love relationship with Jesus, we remove the joy in serving Him. Being His disciple will cost us everything, but it will gain us everything that matters!

As believers, we tend to see the cross primarily as our provision for salvation, and indeed, it is. But it is much more than that. At the cross we find healing and freedom, strength and victory, peace and rest. Kneeling at the cross is our appropriate posture–that of humility, surrender, adoration, and gratitude. We are not strong in ourselves while at the cross; no, we identify with our Lord's weakness and vulnerability. We lay down our self-sufficiency. As we embrace our weaknesses, His strength is infused into us. Jesus said, *"My grace is sufficient for you, for My strength is made perfect in weakness"* **(2 Cor. 12:9)**.

At the cross, we do not race ahead with our ideas and plans; we wait for the Master to reveal His will and ways to us. We do not strategize; we listen. We lay our timetables down and hold tightly to the Eternal One. We gain His perspective and release our own. The cross is our salvation, sanctity, and sanity. It is where we find refreshment and restoration. It's where our lack and needs are intercepted by God's provision. We bring our stress and anxieties, lay them down, and receive His peace. We bring our problems to Jesus and find His solutions.

How dare we neglect the cross?! It is central to our lives! Our past is redeemed, and our future is secured there. At the cross, our hope is rekindled, our joy is restored, and our strength is renewed. Our loneliness is satisfied, and our insecurities alleviated. At the cross our pain is validated. The cross says our pain mattered; it is felt and acknowledged as being significant. The cross sets us free from self-centeredness and trains us for reigning with the Messiah. The path to the cross should be trodden, yes, *well-beaten* by those who are called by the name of the Lord Jesus. May we never tire of the tragedy and majesty of His cross. It must be the center and mainstay of our lives. May we declare like the hymnist: *"In the cross of Christ I glory…!"*

What Did Jesus Provide?

On the cross, Jesus received what we deserved (punishment for sin) and made it possible for us to receive what He deserved (eternal glory). Jesus was wounded (crucified) for our transgressions and sin that we might be forgiven (**Isa. 53:4-5, Col. 2:13-14**). He was made sin with our sinfulness that we might be clothed in His righteousness. He is *Adonai Tsidkenu* (Hebrew)–the Lord our Righteousness! (**Isa. 53:10, 1 Cor. 1:30, 2 Cor. 5:21**)

The cross reveals the gravity of our sin problem. Jesus was bruised and crushed to break the power of iniquity that we might be free from its dictating control. At the cross, we repent of and are delivered from our pride, waywardness, and defensiveness (**Isa. 53:5-7, 11**). We mourn our sin and wretchedness, and we receive His forgiveness.

Romans 8:2 says, *"For the law of the Spirit of life in Christ Jesus has made me free from the law of sin and death."* The Greek word, *eleutheroo*, is the one used for "made free." It means to liberate, set free, and deliver. In the New Covenant, it is used exclusively for Jesus setting man free from the dominion of sin. One of God's covenant names is *Adonai M'kaddesh*–the Lord our Sanctification. He has forgiven our sin and freed us from its power and control!

He was scourged so that we could be healed physically, mentally, and emotionally (**Isa. 53:5; 1 Pet. 2:24; Matt. 8:17**). He bore our griefs, sorrows, sicknesses, and pain (**Isa. 53:4**). He is *Adonai Rophe*–the Lord Who heals (**Ex. 15:26**).

Jesus poured out His soul to death so that we could share in the His life (**Isa. 53:12; Heb. 2:9**). The enemy steals, kills, and destroys, but Jesus offers us an abundant, extraordinary life (**John 10:10**) of joy and peace.

He was made a curse for us so that His many blessings, including Abraham's, are available to us (**Gal. 3:13-14, Deut. 21:22-23**). He took our poverty and gave us His riches, so that we can abound in every good work (**2 Cor. 8:9, 9:8**). Jesus endured our shame that we might share His glory (**Heb. 2:10**). He was rejected, and bore *our* rejection that we might be accepted in His inner circle with the Father, the Holy Spirit, and the family of God (**Isa. 53:3, Eph. 1:3-6**). He came to proclaim the acceptable year of God's grace toward us (**Luke 4:19**).

Jesus was beaten and tortured that we might have peace that passes understanding even while enduring stress, affliction, and adversity. He bore our burdens that we might cast our cares on Him Who cares for us (**1 Pet. 5:7**). He was anointed to heal broken hearts and wounded souls, and to set us free from captivity, oppression, and bondage. He comforts all who mourn, replacing ashes with beauty and mourning with joy. He offers garments of praise to displace spirits of heaviness and their manifestations of rejection, depression, and despair (**Isa. 61:1-3**).

The Cross is for All

The cross is for *all* of us, not only for those who request biblical counseling. All levels of peace, healing, freedom, and sanctification are found there. We need to run to the cross daily!

In recognizing that His blood paid our ransom, we voluntarily, eagerly yield ourselves to Him. As we kneel at that altar, we will find our lives altered by the One Who hung there and rose again to secure all that He died to purchase for us.

The Apostle Andrew, who left Jesus in His hour of trial, when facing his own crucifixion years later, said: *"I would not have preached the honor and glory of the cross if I feared the death of the cross."* Seeing the cross before him, Andrew said, *"O cross, most welcomed and longed for! With a willing mind, joyfully and desirously, I come to you, being the scholar of Him which did hang on you, because I have always been your lover and yearned to embrace you."*

We should desperately desire intimacy not only with the cross Jesus bore, but also with any cross He places upon us. As we shoulder our cross, bowed down under its weight, we identify with His suffering. In that place of brokenness and identification, we experience rich fellowship with Him, such as is unknown to the unbroken and willful. Such intimacy with the Messiah intensifies our love for Him, and enables us to empathize with others in pain.

Not only do we find healing and deliverance at the cross, we also discover that as we view Jesus' terrible sufferings, our own pain comes into perspective. We realize that it is worth it all to intimately know Him, to know His power, and to fellowship with Him in His sufferings. So, like Jesus, we endure the cross and despise the shame for the joy set before us–that of sharing His glory (**Heb. 12:2**)!

"Yet indeed I also count all things loss for the excellence of the knowledge of Christ Jesus my Lord, for whom I have suffered the loss of all things, and count them as rubbish, that I may gain Christ...that I may know Him and the power of His resurrection, and the fellowship of His sufferings, being conformed to His death, if, by any means, I may attain to the resurrection from the dead. Not that I have already attained, or am already perfected; but I press on, that I may lay hold of that for which Christ Jesus has also laid hold of me" (**Phil. 3:8, 10-12**).

APPENDIX A

Practical Guide for a Biblical Counseling Session

Your effectiveness in ministering inner healing to others will largely depend on your private prayer life. Prior to meeting with a counselee, engage in preparatory prayer. Praying alone and/or with your team member(s) will tune you with God's Spirit and enable you to hear Him clearly to follow His lead. Also, the Lord may want to give you privileged information in advance to aid you in how to counsel. Pray for a release of spiritual gifts through you and your team.

Procedure of the Session

1. Set up a time frame. If it's the first session, you may need more than two hours to collect information and begin praying into it. Later sessions are normally shorter than the first one.

2. Open with prayer for guidance, wisdom, and protection against the backlash of the enemy. Pray for God's peaceful, healing presence.

3. Ask opening questions and take notes on the answers:

- Why is she (or he) seeking counsel or help?
- What are the problem areas?
- What is her (his) relationship with God like?
- What are her (his) relationships with significant others like?

Obtain relevant background information that will help you discern and understand the issues. Look and listen for root causes and demonic entry points. Take note of wounds of abuse or rejection. Notice the signs of a rejection or rebellion complex to know what basic sins, behaviors, and temptations may be part of the problem.

4. As you are gathering information, write down what ministry is needed (for prayer later):

- What wounds must be healed?
- Who does he (she) need to forgive?
- What demons must be cast out?
- What entry points need to be confessed, repented of, and closed?
- What essential lies are present?
- What curses or bondages must be broken?
- Where is there a need for repentance?

Spend about half of your session gathering information. Then move toward prayer.

5. Explain how you will pray and make sure the person agrees to cooperate. Explain where she (he) must repent, confess sin, and forgive. Tell him (her) of any demonic involvement you discern and how you'll address those spirits. Explain what can be expected as you cast them out.

The person may need to repeat some prayers after you of repentance and renunciation. Have on hand what you may need for deliverance: a bucket or bowl for vomiting, tissues, water to drink, etc. Pray the truth of God's Word to counteract any lies believed, and release God's blessing after breaking any curses.

6. After your time of prayer and ministry, give the counselee relevant homework:

- Assign Scriptures to read or memorize.
- Give action(s) to take (e.g., to write a letter of apology or read a particular book).
- If the person was delivered from demonic oppression, explain how they can retain their deliverance.
- Suggest biblical instructions for them to walk in victory.

7. Set up a follow-up appointment a week later if needed and possible. At that time, ask:

- Did you do the homework? What has happened since we met?
- How are you now? Do you feel free? Still feel burdened or bound?
- What breakthroughs have you had? What breakthroughs do you need?
- What else do we need to pray about?

APPENDIX B

What God's Word Says about Me

Look up the verses below and memorize as many as you can. Recite them often until they renew the way you believe and think. Use these promises from God's Word as you counsel others.

1. Why should I fear when the Bible says God has not given me *"a spirit of fear, but of power, love, and of a sound mind"* (**2 Tim. 1:7**)?

2. Why should I lack faith to fulfill my calling knowing that God has given to me *"a measure of faith"* (**Rom. 12:3**)?

3. Why should I be weak when the Bible says, *"the Lord is the strength of my life"* (**Ps. 27:1**)?

4. Why should I allow Satan control over my life when He who is in me *"is greater than he who is in the world"* (**1 John 4:4**)?

5. Why should I accept defeat when the Bible says that God always leads me *"in triumph"* (**2 Cor. 2:14**)?

6. Why should I lack wisdom when Jesus became wisdom to me from God, and God gives wisdom to me generously when I ask Him for it (**1 Cor. 1:30, James 1:5**)?

7. Why should I be discouraged when I can remember God's mercy, compassion, and faithfulness (**Lam. 3:21-23**)?

8. Why should I worry when I can cast my anxiety on Jesus Who cares for me (**1 Pet. 5:7**)?

9. Why should I feel condemned when God's Word says there is no condemnation for those who are in Messiah (**Rom. 8:1**)?

10. Why should I feel alone when Jesus said He is with me always and will never leave or forsake me (**Matt. 28:20; Heb. 13:5**)?

11. Why should I feel worthless when Jesus became sin for me that I *"might become the righteousness of God in Him"* (**2 Cor. 5:21**)?

12. Why should I be confused and distressed when God is the author of peace (**1 Cor. 14:33**)?

13. Why should I feel like a failure when I am more than a conqueror in all things through Messiah (**Rom. 8:37**)?

14. Why should I let the pressures of life bother me when I can take courage in knowing that Jesus has *"overcome the world"* and its tribulations (**John 16:33**)?

APPENDIX C

Who Am I in Jesus?

Being in the Messiah is the most critical element of your identity. The list below is made up of verses that state your identity in Jesus. Because you are in Him, every one of these characteristics is true of you. You can make these truths more meaningful, effective, and productive in your life by choosing to believe what God has said. One of the greatest ways to grow into spiritual maturity is to remind yourself of who you are. *No one can consistently live in a manner that is inconsistent with how he perceives himself.* You must see yourself as a child of God in order to live like one.

Look up the verses below and write out what the Bible says about you. Read this list once or twice a day for a while, especially when Satan is trying to deceive you into believing you lack worth and value. The more you affirm who you are in the Messiah, the more your behavior will reflect your true identity.

Matt. 5:13—I am the salt of the earth.

Matt. 5:14 ______________________________

John 1:12 ______________________________

John 5:1, 5 ______________________________

John 15:16 ______________________________

Rom. 6:18, 22 ______________________________

Rom. 8:14, 17 ______________________________

1 Cor. 3:16, 6:19 ______________________________

2 Cor. 5:17, 19 ______________________________

Gal. 3:26, 28 ______________________________

Gal. 4:6-7 ______________________________

Eph. 1:1 ______________________________

Eph. 2:6, 10 ______________________________

Eph. 2:19 ______________________________

Col. 3:12, 1 Thess. 1:4 ______________________________

1 Thess. 5:5 ______________________________

1 Pet. 2:5, 9-11 ______________________________

1 John 3:12 ______________________________

APPENDIX D

Patterns of Iniquity

Read over the lists below, asking the Holy Spirit to reveal to you where you need to confess your iniquity and that of your ancestors. Refer to Chapter 17 for a suggested prayer to use.

List from Isaiah 59

- Hands stained with blood: homicide, blood sacrifices, participating in or greedily watching bullfights, cockfights or dog fights. Abortion. Participating in genocide of ethnic groups.
- Lying tongue: hypocrisy, fraud, deceit
- Wicked tongue: slander, gossip, cursing, mockery, bearing false witness, complaining
- Not crying out for justice: lack of compassion for the less fortunate and refusing to speak up for the helpless and needy. Indifferent to sin within individuals, churches, and cities
- Not judging with truth: showing favoritism to those we love or who profit our cause. Racism. Favoring the rich over the poor, the famous over the unknown.
- Thoughts of iniquity: revenge, plotting evil, resentment, bitterness
- Trusting in vanity, riches, and the systems of this world. Trusting man, medicine, finances, or insurance rather than God
- Walking in unrighteousness: trusting one's own righteousness instead of the Lord's. Making decisions without God's leading. Breaking a commitment, vow, or promise. Causing hurt
- Rebelling against God and His commands: trusting in other gods, idolatry, occultism, witchcraft, New Age, Satanism

List from Exodus 20:1-17 (excluding those already mentioned)

- Taking the name of God in vain: swearing by His name or using it disrespectfully; blasphemy
- Not resting (reveals a lack of trust in God and a refusal to care for His temple, your body)
- Dishonoring parents: not treating them with love; speaking about them unkindly or without respect. Lack of respect for authority

- Adultery: fornication, pornography, sexual perversions, impurity, uncleanness, lust, incest, uncontrolled passions, prostitution
- Stealing: fraud, falsifying measures, paying unjust salaries, tax evasion
- Coveting: lusting after another's spouse or possessions, envy, craving worldly things

List from Galatians 5 (excluding those already mentioned)

- Strife: verbal or physical violence, arguing, jealousy, anger, causing division, sowing discord
- Heresy: changing the context of the Word of God. Twisting Scripture to intimidate or control. Using the Bible for personal gain or to justify sin
- Drunkenness: addiction to drugs or alcohol

List from Colossians 3 (excluding those already mentioned)

- Greed: trusting in riches, idolizing things of this world, usury
- Love of the world. No fear of God. Fearing man, craving approval from man
- Disobedience: to God, His Word, and His authority. Rebellious, independent

List from 2 Timothy 3 (excluding those already mentioned)

- Love of self: vanity, pride, haughtiness, bragging, conceited, egotistical, ungrateful, discontented
- Cruel: sadistic, masochistic, mentally or verbally cruel, merciless
- Loving pleasure more than God
- Corruption, treason, disloyalty

Other common areas of iniquity

- Tempting God: criticizing God or accusing Him
- Profaning what is holy (i.e., abusing one's body through tattoos or excessive body piercings)

APPENDIX E

Deliverance Questionnaire

"Counsel in the heart of man is like deep water, but a man of understanding will draw it out" (**Prov. 20:5**).

When trying to locate the root of a problem, these questions can be helpful and save time.

1. What is troubling you? This question helps a person share what is on his mind and reveal the struggles he's facing.

2. Do you feel loved by God for who you are? Many people do not perceive God as a loving Father. Some believers try hard to earn God's acceptance and approval through performing well even while knowing that salvation is a free gift.

3. What was your relationship with your parents like when you were a child? Children are very sensitive and easily damaged. A rough upbringing can result in unresolved problems later in life. Many areas of bondage begin in childhood. Hurt feelings toward guardians or parents must be confessed and released.

4. What kind of bondage are you experiencing? (e.g., fear, depression, physical illness, hearing voices, mental torment, etc.) It's important to clearly identify the problem, so you know how to deal with it.

5. Do you remember when the bondage started and what was happening? Bondages can often be traced back to a particular experience. If they can remember when the bondage started, they will likely remember what happened that initially triggered the problem. This may reveal the demonic entry point that you can close in prayer.

6. Can you see any open doors where the bondage could have entered? See if they can think of anything. Although they may not know or even be wrong, valuable insight can be given you in the answer to this question.

7. Do you have ancestors or family members who have suffered from a similar problem? This enables you to look at the possibility of a spirit being handed down through a generational curse or iniquity.

8. Have you or your ancestors been involved in the occult or false religions? Many areas of bondage are rooted in some involvement in the occult, either by the person or by their ancestors. False religions are also a common inroad for the enemy. Freemasonry is known for bringing people under demonic bondage.

9. What things have negatively impacted your life? Finding out what has damaged them can reveal the devil's footholds in their lives. Bad relationships often open the door to a root of bitterness. Traumas can result in fear. They may be punishing themselves for sin that they need to confess and forsake. A clean conscience is vital to spiritual freedom.

APPENDIX F

Personal Spiritual Profile

This profile is designed to help people evaluate their upbringing and spiritual background. It is also meant to show how wrong patterns of thinking or behaving may have developed and become a part of who they are. You can use this form as it is for those you pray with, or adapt it to be more suited to you and/or those you counsel.

Please answer each question as truthfully as you can.

Who in your family is a close follower of Jesus?

Have you or anyone in your family been involved in the following?

_____ Hinduism
_____ Baha'i faith
_____ Buddhism
_____ Mormonism
_____ any other cult (which one? _________________)
_____ Free Masons/Shriners
_____ Islam
_____ Jehovah's Witnesses
_____ Christian Science

Have you or anyone in your family been involved in any of the following?

_____ Calling up the dead/spirits
_____ Horoscopes
_____ Palm reading
_____ Fortune-telling
_____ Good luck charms
_____ Demonic videos or games
_____ Out-of-body experiences
_____ Telling the future
_____ Secret order groups
_____ Cults of any type
_____ Use of witchcraft or sorcery
_____ Transcendental meditation
_____ Fascination with occult movies
_____ Worship of any other than the one true God
_____ Psychics
_____ New Age
_____ Ouija boards
_____ Magicians
_____ Yoga
_____ Martial arts
_____ Superstitions

Have any of these tragedies been repetitive in your family?

_____ Plague
_____ Fire
_____ Poverty
_____ Abuse
_____ Incest
_____ Murder
_____ Divorce
_____ Financial ruin
_____ Rape

Are you aware of the existence of any ancestral sins, such as these?

_____ Violence
_____ Alcohol abuse
_____ Sexual immorality
_____ Sexual abuse
_____ Drug abuse
_____ Adultery

Were there major sins committed against you in your childhood by a family member or someone else?

_____ Sexual abuse
_____ Verbal abuse
_____ Abandonment
_____ Physical abuse
_____ Rejection

With what areas of obedience to God's Word do you habitually struggle?

_____ Prayer
_____ Meditation
_____ Self-control
_____ Faith
_____ Fasting
_____ Growing in Christ-likeness
_____ Tithing
_____ Submission to authority
_____ Fellowshipping with believers
_____ Supernatural work of the Holy Spirit

Have you ever participated in or been a part of any of these sexual sins?

_____ Fornication
_____ Homosexuality
_____ Lust
_____ Masturbation
_____ Sexual fantasizing
_____ Telephone/cyber sex
_____ Exhibitionism (wanting others to see your nakedness)
_____ Adultery
_____ Molestation
_____ Incest
_____ Bestiality (sex w/animals
_____ Pornography
_____ Desire to see others' nakedness

Do you have any of the following addictive/destructive habits?

_____ Sleeping disorders
_____ Forgetfulness
_____ Illegal drug abuse
_____ Smoking
_____ Envy/jealousy
_____ Manipulation
_____ Frequent tardiness
_____ Excessive computer play
_____ Addiction to video games
_____ Being argumentative
_____ Obsessive indulgences
_____ Seductive behavior
_____ Dirty language
_____ Excessive foolish talking
_____ Stealing
_____ Alcohol addiction
_____ Prescription drug abuse
_____ Violence
_____ Lying
_____ Eating disorders
_____ Breaking promises
_____ Bad attitudes
_____ Gambling
_____ Adult movies
_____ Addiction to TV
_____ Selfishness/greed
_____ Disorganization
_____ Mocking spiritual things

Do you habitually experience any of these dispositions, emotions, or thoughts?

_____ Anxiety/fear
_____ Anger
_____ Being critical of others
_____ Perfectionism
_____ Feeling of inferiority
_____ Rationalizing
_____ Lengthy depression
_____ Bitterness
_____ Confusion
_____ Apathy
_____ Loneliness/isolation
_____ Pride/superiority
_____ Indecisiveness
_____ Racism
_____ Hatred of someone (Who? ___________)
_____ Unforgiveness (Toward whom? _____________)

Do you regularly experience any of these spiritual encounters?

_____ Nightmares
_____ Premonitions
_____ Fearful/unclean thoughts
_____ Demonic visitations
_____ De'ja vu experiences
_____ Demonic visions
_____ Demonic/driving thoughts in your mind

Do you have any of the following problems preventing you from having a normal healthy condition?

_____ Chronic illnesses
_____ External problems
_____ Low energy levels
_____ Attention deficit disorder
_____ Internal organ problems
_____ Dyslexia
_____ Major disease(s)
_____ Sense impairment

Give a brief answer to describe the following

- Your relationship with your mother:
- Your relationship with your father:
- Your relationship with your children:
- Your relationship with your spouse (if married):
- Your relationship with any other significant individuals in your life:
- Your social life:

What is the one thing you hoped would not be asked in this questionnaire?

Curses, Vows, and Judgments

Curses are words spoken against you by someone. They are often in response to rebellion against authority (**Gen. 3:14-17, Mark 11:20-21**). Have you any knowledge of curses at work in your life, past or present, such as spoken by teachers, bosses, public leaders, or spiritual leaders?

Vows and oaths are promises or pledges made. Have you any knowledge of vows or oaths at work in your life, past or present, including words spoken by you (Example: "If it takes every penny I have, I'll get even with you.")?

Judgments are negative conclusions about a person that are projected into his future. Usually these are precipitated by the person's condition or performance (**Matt. 18:18**). Do you know of any judgments made against you, past or present? (Example: "You are stupid." "You'll never be successful.")

APPENDIX G

Evil Spirits in the Bible and Their Manifestations

Spirit of heaviness: Isaiah 61:3

- To mourn, be grieved or bruised (**Luke 4:18**), to despair
- Unbelief, gluttony, rejection, self-pity (**Ps. 69:20**), hopelessness; suicidal thoughts
- Sadness, depression (**Prov. 15:13**), loneliness, discouragement, and gloominess

Spirit of infirmity: Luke 13:11

- Frail, impotent, weak, feeble
- Pain or illness that cannot be diagnosed; a lingering disorder
- Some back problems, headaches, sugar diabetes, heart disease, hay fever, fungus, fever, viral infections, sinus infections, and arthritis

Note: The spirit of infirmity is often passed down from one generation to another. A spirit of heaviness can weaken the immune system and make a person more susceptible to a spirit of infirmity.

Spirit of bondage: Romans 8:15

- All addictions (chemicals, cigarettes, alcohol, entertainment, food, sex, relationships, work, gadgets, internet, etc.)
- Bitterness, fear, greed, ambition, and lust
- Compulsory sin (**Prov. 5:22**)
- Satanic captivity, oppression (**2 Tim. 2:26**)
- Being under another's power and dominion; unhealthy soul ties, and co-dependency

Spirit of haughtiness: Proverbs 16:18-19

- Arrogant, egotistical, proud (**Prov. 6:16-17**), disrespectful
- Self-righteous, brags or boasts, gossips or slanders, scorns or mocks
- Stiff-necked, stubborn, rude, vain, dictatorial, and insolent
- Controlling, angry, contentious, and argumentative (**Prov. 13:10**)

Spirit of fear: 2 Timothy 1:7

- Anxious, apprehensive, timid, and unduly cautious
- To be tormented, to tremble (**Job 4:14-15**; **Ps. 55:5**), to be faithless
- To feel overly shy, intimidated, inferior, inadequate, tense, stressed, and agitated
- May cause heart attacks, fear of death (**Heb. 2:14-15**), nightmares
- Phobias (paralyzing fear of the dark, water, heights, etc.); fear of man; fear of poverty

Lying spirit: 2 Chronicles 18:22

- Lies, deception, strong delusion
- False impressions (**2 Thess. 2:11**); religious spirits
- Exaggeration, flattery, gossip, hypocrisy, accusation, profanity, and condemnation

Deceiving spirit: 1 Tim 4:1

- False doctrines, cults, heresies

Perverse spirit: Isaiah 19:14

[Perverse = to bend, twist, distort, or lead astray. (**Prov. 11:20**)]

- Connected to lust, sexual perversions and deviations, prostitution, and homosexuality
- Error (**Isa. 19:14**); rebellious, false teachers who twist the Word (**2 Pet. 2**); lovers of self
- Causes hatred toward God (**Prov. 14:2**) and one to be despised by others
- Perverts and misinterprets the gospel

Note: A perverse spirit often attaches to a wounded spirit, which is often caused by rejection (**Prov. 15:4**).

Spirit of jealousy: Numbers 5:14

- Jealousy, competition, covetousness, strife (divides congregation and homes)
- Anger, murder (**Gen. 4:4-8**), rage, revenge (**Prov. 6:34**), hatred (**Gen. 37:3-8**)
- Cruel (**Song of Sol. 8:6**), suspicious, envious, selfish

<u>Spirit of divination</u>: Acts 16:16

- Fortune-telling, water witching, witchcraft, ESP, necromancy
- Divination (to obtain secret knowledge, especially of the future)
- Hypnotism

<u>Antichrist spirit</u>: 1 John 4:3

- Religious, murderous spirit (persecutes believers)
- Legalism; tries to seduce into error
- Attempts to displace God and enthrone self
- Targets the anointing; especially tries to destroy prophets
- Opposes priestly office of Messiah and believers

<u>Spirit of harlotry</u>: Hosea 4:12, 5:4

- Unfaithfulness, prostitution, adultery; rebellion
- Idolatrous love of the world, status, money, and/or food

<u>Spirit of deep sleep (slumbering spirit)</u>: Isaiah 29:10-13

- Makes the Bible hard to understand; unbelief
- Tries to keep a person from yielding to God; prevents intimacy with Him
- Makes a person feel sleepy during worship services or when reading God's Word
- Causes one to easily forget what he heard or read in the Scriptures

<u>Deaf and dumb spirit</u>: Mark 9:25-26

- Dumbness, inner ear diseases, blindness, eye diseases (not caused by aging process)
- Lunacy, epilepsy, convulsions, seizures, gnashing of teeth; compels and drives
- Suicidal tendencies; madness, insanity, can cause hydrophobia or schizophrenia

APPENDIX H

The Baptism with the Holy Spirit

Both the public ministry of Jesus and the public ministry of the early Church began with a life-changing encounter with the Holy Spirit. The power of the Spirit in Jesus' life authorized Him to preach the kingdom of God and to demonstrate the kingdom by healing the sick, casting out demons, and raising the dead. The same power and authority was given to the disciples in Acts 2. Jesus Christ is the *prototype* of the Spirit-filled, Spirit-empowered life. The Book of Acts tells of the disciples receiving what Jesus received in order to do what He did.

The purpose of the outpouring of the Holy Spirit was to empower the Body of Messiah for ministry. The author of Acts describes the release of the Holy Spirit with a variety of terms: they were *filled* with the Spirit (2:4, 9:17); they *received* the Holy Spirit (8:17); the Holy Spirit *fell* on them (10:44); the Holy Spirit was *poured out* on them (10:45); the Holy Spirit *came upon* them (19:6). Three of these five instances record that they spoke in tongues. One time, they prophesied *and* spoke in tongues. A fourth time there was evidence that they received this gift, but we are not told what the evidence was.

Jesus' final words in Matthew 28:18-20, Mark 16:15-18, Luke 24:46-49, and John 21:15-17 were commissions for His disciples to preach the gospel, to feed and tend His people, and to make disciples of all nations. In Luke 24, Jesus said, *"Don't go without the power! You can't do this in your own strength! You need the promise of the Father!"*

Being baptized with the Spirit (*see* **Acts 1:4-5**) is not the same experience as described in John 20:22 when Jesus breathed on His men and said, *"Receive the Holy Spirit."* That was the new birth Jesus spoke of in John 3:5. In the timing of John 20, Jesus had purchased salvation, but had not yet ascended to the Father. The baptism of the Spirit could only come *after* His ascension (*see* **John 7:39**).

In John 7, the Jews were celebrating *Succot*, the Feast of Tabernacles. Each day during the Feast of Tabernacles, a celebration of joy was observed where the priests brought water to the Temple from the pool of Siloam in a golden pitcher. The water was poured out on the altar as an offering to God, while the people shouted and sang. Jesus, the fulfillment of this ceremony, cried out, *"If anyone is thirsty, let him come to Me and drink. He who believes in Me...out of his heart will flow rivers of living water"* (**John 7:37-38**).

Jesus used the word "rivers," which contrasts with the word "fountain" found in John 4:14. The new birth is called a *fountain* of living water that springs up within us, resulting in everlasting life. The Holy Spirit is called *rivers* of living water. When we are immersed into God's Spirit, this fountain becomes a river that overflows its banks through us. It's not a stream, but *rivers* of water, like a dam breaking. Isaiah prophesied, *"For I will pour water on him who is thirsty, and floods on the dry ground; I will pour My Spirit on your descendants, and My blessing on your offspring"* (**Isa. 44:3**).

In Matthew 3:11, John the Baptist said the coming Messiah would baptize with the Holy Spirit and fire. We see the fulfillment of this when in Acts 2:1-4 the disciples were praying together, waiting for the promise of the Father. The Holy Spirit settled upon each of them in the form of "tongues of fire." As they were baptized with the Spirit, they began to speak in unknown tongues. At this time, there were devout Jews in Jerusalem from every nation because it was the Feast of *Shavuot*, the Feast of Weeks (*see* **Num. 28:26**). These men heard the disciples speaking in their national languages glorifying God. The miracle might have been in the speaking or in the hearing or in both. They spoke in tongues unknown to them, but the crowd heard them speak in their own languages.

What about speaking in tongues?

Psalm 12:4 says that whoever is lord over us is revealed by who masters our tongue. He who controls the tongue is master of all. *"If any man offend not in word, the same is a perfect man, and able also to bridle the whole body"* (**James 3:2**).

1 Corinthians 14:2, 4-5 says that tongues is a language of the Spirit that aids us in prayer and edifies us. Because it is directed to God, it does not need to be interpreted. The Holy Spirit knows the heart and will of God and helps us pray accordingly.

There is *another* gift of tongues mentioned in 1 Corinthians 12:7-11. This gift of tongues is a message from God to the Church and requires interpretation so that believers can be edified (see **1 Cor. 14:12-19**).

The basic difference between the prayer language of the Spirit and the gift of different kinds of tongues is directional. Who initiates the communication and to whom it is directed? The prayer language (or tongues) is from us to God. We use it in prayer and worship. *We* initiate using this gift, and there is no need for an interpretation. The gift of different kinds of tongues is from God to us. It is to edify the Church. It is initiated by *God*, used in public gatherings, and must be interpreted.

We who want to serve the Lord are in the same situation as His early followers. We hear Jesus' commissions to preach the gospel and make disciples, and we want to obey. And He says to us as He said to them, *"Don't try to do what I've called you to do without the power of the Holy Spirit! Wait until you are endued with power from on high!"*

To receive the Baptism with the Spirit

1. Be born again of the Spirit. Have you surrendered your life to Jesus? (**John 3:5**)
2. Be thirsty! Are you aware that you need greater measures of God's power and anointing in your life? (**John 7:37**)
3. Ask Jesus to baptize you with His Spirit and fire. (**Matt. 3:11**)
4. Confess as sin, repent of, and renounce involvement in the occult or false religions.
5. Forgive anyone who has hurt, abused or disappointed you.
6. Release any unforgiveness toward God and/or yourself. Receive His forgiveness and cleansing.
7. Receive this gift by faith and with thanks, knowing the Lord wants to give it to you. (**Luke 11:13**)

What can you expect?

The Holy Spirit will come upon you and be released through you. You may feel emotions (crying, laughing…), and you may not. If you have inner wounds in your soul, you might feel the Holy Spirit healing those wounds; you might weep before you feel a release of joy and peace. You may feel baptized in love, as many testify. Some people feel the power of the Spirit so strongly that they fall down under the weight of it and lay quietly for a while as His peace enfolds them. You might speak in tongues or prophesy or both. You may do neither initially, but do ask the Lord to release your tongue so that you can use this precious gift. Acts 2:4 says *they* spoke with other tongues as the *Spirit* gave them utterance. So *He* gives the prayer language, and we use *our mouth* and *lips* to speak in the unknown tongue.

Praying for others to receive

When you pray with those who want to receive the baptism with the Holy Spirit, make sure they understand this gift. You might want to teach them from this Appendix and from Chapter Six. When they are ready and hungry to receive, use the points above as you pray. After they have made sure their hearts are clean through confession and have renounced all involvement in the occult, they can ask Jesus to baptize them with His Holy Spirit.

If it is possible, lay your hands on them while you pray for them to receive the baptism with the Spirit. You can pray Scriptures like Luke 11:13 and John 7:38. It is helpful for those receiving to hear you praying freely in the Spirit. It gives them the boldness to begin to exercise the gift of tongues, too. If they don't receive a prayer language right away, you can suggest that they worship God in the privacy of their home, raising their hands, and kneeling in humility. That posture positions one to receive from the Lord more easily. They will probably find that soon their mother tongue is insufficient to express the love in their heart, and they will automatically move into a language of the Spirit. Some people receive tongues while going about their normal lives, e.g., while doing yard work, housework, or even while sleeping.

Be Filled with the Spirit

There are times when we must be refilled with God's Spirit. We need it when we have been complacent and haven't exercised the gifts of the Spirit. We need it when we have preached to or served others, and we feel weary. We need it when we lack boldness to witness for Jesus.

Ephesians 5:18b says literally in Greek, *"Be being filled..."* We are to be continually filled with the Spirit through singing, worshiping with music, giving thanks, and submitting to one another (see **Eph. 5:19-21**). The Holy Spirit should influence all aspects of our lives, resulting in transformed relationships, dynamic ministry, and enhanced worship. When you feel depleted, be filled *again* with the Holy Spirit!

Bibliography

Adams, Jay E. *Competent to Counsel.* Grand Rapids, MI: Baker Book House, 1978. Print.

Allender, Dr. Dan B. *The Wounded Heart.* Colorado Springs, CO: NavPress, 1995. Print.

Basham, Don. *Can a Christian Have a Demon?* Monroeville, PN: Whitaker Books, 1971. Print.

Bevere, John. *Breaking Intimidation.* Lake Mary, FL: Creation House, 1995. Print.

Bevere, John. *The Bait of Satan: Your Response Determines Your Future.* Orlando, FL: Creation House, 1995. Print.

Bridges, Jerry. *Trusting God Even When Life Hurts.* Colorado Springs, CO: NavPress, 1988. Print.

Chafer, Lewis Sperry. *Satan, His Motives and Methods.* Grand Rapids, MI: Kregal, 1991. Print.

Clinebell, Howard J. JR. *Basic Types of Pastoral Counseling.* Nashville, TN: Abingdon, 1966. Print.

Cramer, Raymond L. *The Psychology of Jesus and Mental Health.* Grand Rapids, MI: Zondervan, 1977. Print.

Crossland, Don. *A Journey Towards Wholeness.* Nashville, TN: StarSong, 1991. Print.

Ferrell, Ana Mendez. *Iniquity,* Ponte Verda, Florida: E & A International, 1960. Print.

Gardner, Thom. *Healing the Wounded Heart.* Shippensgurg, PA: Destiny Image Publishers, Inc., 2005. Print.

Jones, Russell Bradley, *Gold from Golgotha*, Grand Rapids, MI: Baker Book House, 1957. Print.

Kylstra, Chester and Betsy. *Restoring the Foundations*, Video series.

Lerm, Adriana and Ross, Reuven and Yanit. *Relating to An Awesome God*, Andalucia, AL: Write Hand Publishing, 2008. Print.

Hickey, Marilyn, *Breaking Generational Curses*, 2001. Tulsa, OK: Harrison House, Inc. Print.

Horrobin, Peter. *Healing Through Deliverance.* England: St. Ives Plc, 1995. Print.

Mayhall, Carole. *Words That Hurt; Words That Heal.* Colorado Springs, CO: NavPress, 1990. Print.

Ogilvie, Lloyd John. *Autobiography of God.* Ventura, CA: Regal Books, 1984. Print.

Prince, Derek. *They Shall Expel Demons*. Grand Rapids, MI: Chosen Books, 1998. Print.

Prince, Derek. *God's Remedy for Rejection.* Orlando, Florida: Christian Life Books, 1993. Print.

Prince, Derek. *Life's Bitter Pool.* Ft. Lauderdale, FL: Derek Prince, 1984. Print.

Sandford, John and Paula. *The Transformation of the Inner Man*. Plainfield, NJ: Bridge Publishing, Inc. 1982. Print.

Sandford, John and Paula. *Healing the Wounded Spirit.* Tulsa, OK: Victory House, Inc. 1985. Print.

Seamands, David. *Healing for Damaged Emotions*. Wheaten, IL: Victor Books, 1985. Print.

Sides, Dale M. *Understanding & Breaking the Schemes of the Devil.* Bedford, VA: Liberating Ministries for Christ International, 2003. Print.

Snanoudj, Sergine. *To Loose the Chains*. Jasper, AR: End-Time Handmaidens, 1981. Print.

Smalley, Gary, and Dr. John Trent. *The Two Sides of Love*. Pomona, CA: Focus on the Family. 1990. Print.

Sorge, Bob. *Dealing with the Rejection and Praise of Man*. Lee's Summit, MO: Oasis House, 2000. Print.

Stone, Perry. *Purging your House, Pruning your Family Tree*. Lake Mary, FL: Charisma House, 2011. Print.

Sumrall, Lester. *Demons; The Answer Book.* Nashville, TN: Thomas Nelson Publishers, 1979. Print.

Thompson, Carroll. *Possess the Land!* Dallas, TX: Carroll Thompson Ministries, 1977. Print.

Thompson, Dr. Bruce, and Barbara Thompson. *Walls of My Heart*. Euclid, MN: Crown Ministries International, 1989. Print.

Tapscott, Betty. *Set Free Through Inner Healing*. Humble, TX: Hunter Books, 1978. Print.

Tapscott, Betty. *Ministering Inner Healing Biblically.* Houston, TX: Tapscott Ministries, 1987. Print.

Made in the USA
Lexington, KY
01 August 2017